Unleash Your
INNER SUPER POWERS

Unleash Your
INNER SUPER POWERS

AND DESTROY FEAR AND SELF-DOUBT

Book 3 of 3 from the

Words of Wisdom for Teens Series

Jacqui Letran

A Healed Mind

ASHEVILLE, NC

Cover Image: Stephanie DePass Designs

Names: Letran, Jacqui.
Title: Unleash Your Inner Super Powers: and destroy fear and self-doubt/ Jacqui Letran.
Description: 1st edition. | Asheville, North Carolina: A Healed Mind, [2016] | Series: Words of wisdom for teens series ; book 3 | Interest age level: 12 and up.
Identifiers: ISBN 978-0-9976244-6-5 | ISBN 978-0-9976244-5-8 (ebook)
Subjects: LCSH: Adolescent psychology. | Teenagers--Attitudes. | Happiness in adolescence. | Emotions in adolescence. | Self-help techniques for teenagers.

Contents

Introduction

Do you often feel as though other people are better than you? Does it seem they are more carefree, more outgoing, and more confident? They make friends easily and good things seem to happen for them all the time. They are fun, witty, and full of charm. Everywhere they go, people are drawn to them. They do what they want and say what they think.

These positive, likable traits seem to come so naturally for them. But for you, life is filled with anxiety, fear, and self-doubt. What is their secret? How can they talk to anyone about anything with ease, while it's a significant struggle for you to just be in the presence of others, let alone carry on a conversation?

You dream of being different. You dream of being comfortable in your own skin. You dream of creating meaningful relationships, going after what you want with confidence, and feeling happy and satisfied with your everyday life. But your fear and self-doubt are holding you back, causing you to feel trapped and powerless to change your situation. You're left feeling sad, lonely, and insecure about yourself and your life.

What if there was a way to change all of that? What if you could destroy your fear and self-doubt and be strong and self-assured instead? What would it be like if you could go into any situation with excitement, courage, and confidence? Imagine what your life would look like and what you would be able to achieve. Just imagine.

I'm going to let you in on a little secret. That excitement, courage, and confidence which you admire in others are skills that are learned.

Sure, there are some people for whom these traits come naturally, but if you were not born with these traits, you can learn them. The thing is, you can learn to destroy your fear and self-doubt and go after whatever you want with confidence. You can learn to be comfortable in your own skin and be completely at ease while expressing yourself.

You were born with all the resources—or Inner Super Powers (ISPs)—you need to be happy, resilient, and successful in life. The problem is you have not been aware of these ISPs, nor how to use them.

Maybe you saw a glimpse of them here and there, but you didn't recognize their power or have faith in them. If you don't know what your ISPs are, how can you tap into them consistently and achieve the results that you want and deserve?

In this book, you will learn:
- The seven Inner Super Powers guaranteed to destroy your fear and self-doubt
- How to connect to and strengthen your Inner Super Powers

- How to consistently tap into and unleash your Inner Super Powers whenever you want to
- How to live within your full power and be happy, confident, and successful in life—and so much more!

You have so many Inner Super Powers that make you wonderful in every way. In this book, I have chosen to share seven specific ISPs because these seven are your best bet for destroying fear and self-doubt.

There is much written about each of these ISPs and each ISPs can be a stand-alone book. However, I know your time is valuable and you have other responsibilities and activities to tend to. This is why you'll find that these chapters are brief and to the point.

I will present enough information for you to understand your ISPs without bogging you down with too much information. By reading this book and completing the activities within each section, you will learn how to consistently tap into these ISPs, to harness them, and unleash them whenever you want. You can learn how to confidently go after what you want and create that happy and successful life you've been dreaming about.

> **NOTE:** To get the most benefit from this book, do work on each Inner Super Power in the order presented, as the concepts of each build to the next.

CHAPTER 1

It's All in Your Mind

Your mind has everything to do with your Inner Super Powers. It is essential for you to understand how your mind works so you can truly tap into them.

> In this book, I will give you a brief overview of the inner workings of your mind. If you would like to go deeper into this topic, you can read the second book in this series, entitled *I would, but my DAMN MIND won't let me*, where this topic is discussed in more depth.

Your Conscious and Subconscious Mind

Your conscious mind is your logical mind. It's the part of your mind that you are aware of. It's the part of your mind that you use when you focus on things or learn something new.

For example, your conscious mind helps you to learn how to play a sport, such as tennis. When you are in the learning phase, you consciously focus on learning proper techniques, such as how to hold the racquet properly, how to position your body in preparation for the incoming ball, and the proper way to move your body to create an effective swing. These thoughts and actions are the work of your conscious mind—something you are aware of and actively focusing on.

Your conscious mind is also responsible for helping you make decisions based on the things that are in front of you and the things that you've learned from previous experiences. It is the part of your mind that makes simple decisions such as, "I want to wear shorts today because it's a warm day."

It also makes more complex decisions such as, "Should I lie to my mom so I can get out of trouble, but risk having her find out and getting even more upset with me?"

Your conscious mind does not work fully until around seven years old. This is why you believed in the Tooth Fairy, the Easter Bunny, and Santa Claus (not to mention your imaginary best friend) when you were a little kid. Before seven, you don't have a fully working logical mind that says, "That's not true because I've learned so-and-so and that doesn't match what I've learned."

As you get older and your conscious mind develops more and more, you begin to question whether those beliefs are true. Eventually, you stop believing in the Tooth Fairy, the Easter Bunny, and Santa Claus because your conscious mind is fully-formed and you can logically make decisions based on the facts you have learned over the years.

Your subconscious mind is very different from your conscious mind. The first important difference is that you are not aware of, nor can you control, what happens in your subconscious mind. Everything that happens in the subconscious part of your mind is happening without you knowing and without your control. In fact, everything that happens in your subconscious mind happens automatically, as if it's a program running on autopilot in the background.

Your subconscious mind works immediately at birth and one of its biggest jobs is to keep you alive and safe. However, to the subconscious mind, "safe" doesn't necessarily mean "safe" the way you probably define it today. Instead, "safe" means "Do not change. Stay exactly the way you are. Change is scary. Change is dangerous. If you try to change, you will get hurt."

When you are doing something new or outside of your belief system, your subconscious mind freaks out. It believes that you are putting yourself at risk for failure, rejection, or pain. So, it will do whatever it can to get you back to your "safe" place, which means going back to your old ways and staying exactly how you are right now.

To get you back to your "safe" place, your subconscious mind uses fear tactics to prevent you from taking actions and moving forward. It will do whatever it needs to do to get you to stop doing that new activity and return you to where you were. This is why a lot of people report feeling "stuck" when they are dealing with unhappy or difficult situations.

How many times have you wanted to do something, especially something new and a little scary, and immediately started feeling anxious and full of self-doubt? Even though you really wanted to do that thing, all you could think of is how you could end up failing, hurting, or embarrassing yourself. So, instead of following through and doing what you initially wanted to do, you stop and retreat to your familiar pattern.

That's your subconscious mind at work. Your subconscious mind knows that when you are fearful or anxious, chances are you will stop what you're thinking about doing or attempting to do and go back to your old ways, the "safe" and familiar ways. Every time you do attempt something and retreat back to your old patterns, you reinforce your beliefs of "I can't" or "This is who I am."

Your Subconscious Mind Simplified

Let's explore your subconscious mind a little more; once you understand how your subconscious mind works, it will be so much easier to access your Inner Super Powers.

First, I want you to think of your subconscious mind as a collection of movies within a movie library. In this movie library, there are hundreds of thousands of movies—all starring YOU! Imagine there's a DVD for everything you have ever thought, felt, or done. That's a lot of DVDs, isn't it?

In your movie library is your personal assistant, which is really your subconscious mind. Its job is to continue to record your movies, store them, and replay them at the right time for you. In addition, your subconscious mind has a bigger job: to keep you safe. Unfortunately, more often than not, that means creating anxiety, fear, and self-doubt to prevent you from moving into the perceived unsafe territory.

Also, your subconscious mind is programmed to give you whatever experience you're looking for in the easiest, quickest way possible. Yes, you read that right! Your subconscious mind is programmed to give you whatever experience you're looking for, in the easiest, quickest way possible—as long as the thing you want matches your belief system. How you have perceived all of your experiences so far has been because of the requests you have made to your subconscious mind.

You might be thinking, "But I didn't ask for all the stress or pain that I'm experiencing, nor for all those judgments I've been receiving."

While it might not seem like you've asked for those experiences, you did. You didn't know that you were asking for them because you don't fully understand how your mind works, or the enormous potential of your Inner Super Powers yet. (Hint: They are the key to radically changing how you ask for future experiences!).

Let me explain how you've been asking your mind for your experiences so far. Every single thought and feeling you have is a direct command to your subconscious mind: "This is the experience I want to have. Give me this experience."

Therefore, when you were getting ready for that presentation in class and you imagined how nervous you're going to be when it's your turn to stand up and present, you gave your subconscious mind these commands: "I want to be nervous during the presentation. This is the experience that I want. Give me this experience. Make sure I'm nervous during the presentation."

Being a loyal and faithful assistant, your subconscious mind goes to work immediately and begins to scan your environment, searching for anything that could cause you to be nervous. The moment it finds something that could result in you feeling nervous, it directs all your attention to that thing.

At the same time, your subconscious mind will look into your movie library, looking for past movies that could cause you to feel nervous about your current situation. It will replay those movies for you automatically in the background of your mind. In addition, it creates a new movie of what could possibly happen in your future based on your past experiences and the current experience you're asking for.

Not only does your subconscious replay all the times you were nervous presenting in front of the class, but it also starts playing the new movie it just made of you stumbling on your words and failing miserably during your presentation today. By the time it's your turn to present, you have become so nervous that all you can focus on is the sweatiness of your palms, the shakiness of your voice, and all those judgmental looks from your classmates.

The good news is that once you understand your subconscious mind and your Inner Super Powers, you can purposefully send the right commands to your subconscious mind in a positive and powerful way. That way, your subconscious mind can bring you a much better experience than what you have been through in the past.

A moment ago, I mentioned that your subconscious mind's job is to give you the experience you're looking for as long as it matches your current belief system. Your belief system is the program of your subconscious mind that runs on autopilot in the background. Whatever you believe is true is what your subconscious mind will continuously look for evidence of.

Similar to the concept that all thoughts and feelings are direct commands to your subconscious mind ("This is the experience I want; give me this experience."), your belief systems are also direct commands. However, belief systems are even more powerful because they run automatically in the background of your mind all day long. You don't even have to actively request these experiences through your thoughts and feelings.

As humans, we have this need to be right and our subconscious mind will work hard to make sure that this need is fulfilled. To complete this task, your subconscious mind will generalize, distort, or delete details so that the only experiences you have will match your belief system.

For example, if you have a belief that you are forgetful, your subconscious mind will ignore each instance of you remembering details, or will distort it and call it "pure luck" or "a coincidence" when you catch yourself remembering something. The fact is, you remember so much more than you forget, but when you forget something, your subconscious mind will happily bring it to your awareness.

Another example of how your subconscious mind will make sure your experiences match your beliefs is through generalization. Let's say you were bitten by a dog when you were young and that experience caused you significant pain and fear. To protect you from another similar painful episode, your mind might create the generalization that "all dogs are mean and will bite you." This causes you to hate dogs and you find yourself feeling fearful whenever you're around any dog.

Unfortunately, dogs are great at picking up on when someone doesn't like them or when someone is fearful of them. To protect themselves, dogs will act aggressively when you are nearby because they sense your dislike and fear. This generalization allows you to be right and even influences the world around you (a dog in this case) to provide you with the experience that "all dogs are mean," when in fact, most dogs are rather sweet.

Commanding Your Subconscious Mind

Just a moment ago, you learned that every thought you have and every feeling you feel is a command to your subconscious mind to give you more of the same experience.

Here are three more important details for you to effectively command your mind:

Negative Commands Confuse Your Mind

Your subconscious mind does not know how to process negative commands. Negative commands are commands such as, "I don't want" or "I'm no longer" or "I'm not." Basically, they are any command that focuses on what you are *not*, or what you *don't* want. This is because, for your subconscious mind to fully understand your command, it has to be able to create a picture or to clearly see the experience you're looking for.

Let's say you wanted your brother to bring you your blue sweater and you said to him, "Can you go to my room and bring me my sweater? I don't want the orange one." What are the chances that your brother would know you want him to bring you the *blue* sweater? Pretty slim—unless of course, you only have two sweaters, an orange one and a blue one. Even then, wouldn't it be better to say to him, "Bring me the blue sweater," so he knows what color to look for and can find it quickly for you? Your subconscious mind works the same way. When you give the command, "I don't want to be sad," it might seem like a good command at first because you don't want to be sad. But that command doesn't help your mind to clearly understand your true request. All it knows is that you don't want the experience of being sad, but it has no idea of what experience you want instead. Your subconscious mind doesn't know if you want to feel angry, overwhelmed, unmotivated, disgusted, or any number of other feelings.

To help your subconscious mind understand your command, it creates a picture for each of the words in the command that can have an associated image, which are "I" and "sad" in this instance. The mental picture of this command is, therefore, an image of you being sad. Then, the command becomes, "I want to be sad."

This is why it is so important to focus on what you want, rather than what you don't want. If you gave the command, "I want to be happy," or "I want to be relaxed," your subconscious mind would understand that clearly and could bring that to you easily.

Weak Versus Strong Commands
The commands that you give your subconscious mind can be viewed as strong or weak commands. Strong commands get your subconscious mind's attention immediately and direct your subconscious mind effectively.

One way to think about this is by knowing that you are the boss of your mind. As a boss, you can be firm or weak with your commands. To effectively command your subconscious mind and get your desired results, choose strong, powerful commands. Commands such as, "I choose," "I'm ready," "I'm determined," or "I'm committed to," are very strong commands.

Think about it. When you say, "I am determined to be an A student," how does that look in your mind's eye? How does that feel?

Now, try for the same outcome, but with a weaker command. "I hope I'll be an A student." How is this picture different in your mind? How does this command make you feel?

In the "determined" picture, you are in charge of your outcome. Chances are you'll see yourself confidently going after what you want to achieve. You might see yourself putting energy and effort into studying. You might see yourself pushing through barriers to achieve success.

In the "hope" picture, you might see yourself as uncertain as you attempt to work toward your goal. The energy and effort you're putting into those activities are not as strong or as persistent as your "determined" picture. Sure, you may do some of the work, but you'll leave more to chance.

Weak commands to avoid are commands such as, "I wish," "I want," or "I hope." When you wish, want, or hope for a result, your attitude about how to proceed isn't as solid or as powerful as when you are ready, determined, or committed to your goal.

Vague Comparative Commands Don't Help

Your subconscious mind is very literal, which could cause it to believe that it has successfully given you the experiences you've asked for when, in fact, it hasn't. When you give your subconscious mind a Vague Comparative Command that sounds like, "I wish I had more money," the "more money" part of that sentence is a comparison of one thing to another. Yet, it doesn't really identify what it's being compared to.

What does "more money" mean, exactly? More money than you've had in your life? More money than whom? If you had one penny more than you did a minute ago, you do, in fact, have more money, but I doubt that's what your intention was when you made the request.

Now, if you said, "I am determined to have $100 more than I have right now," your subconscious mind knows exactly what you want, doesn't it?

Suppose you give your subconscious mind the command, "I want to be happier." Again, happier than when? Happier than whom? To your subconscious mind, if you are happier now than you were last week (when you were overwhelmingly depressed), then it would believe that it has already successfully delivered the experience you're asking for and it doesn't have to do anything else other than to continue to give you the same experience.

Strong, powerful, and clear commands such as, "I am committed to being happy," or "I'm ready to be happy," are great alternatives. When you use these commands, your subconscious mind will get busy looking for reasons for why you should be happy in that moment and evidence that you are committed to your happiness.

REMEMBER: To give your subconscious mind the most powerful commands, always:

1. Focus on the outcome you want and be specific.

2. Avoid focusing on the thing that you don't want, or the condition you want to move away from.

3. Use strong command words such as "choose," "ready to," "committed to," and "determined to."

4. Avoid Vague Comparative Commands such as "more" or "better than." If you give a comparative command, it is best to give a specific comparison.

Stop Watching Those Crappy Movies

Think of a type of movie that you absolutely hate to watch because it's uncomfortable or it stresses you out. For me, it's gory, violent movies. For the sake of this example, let's pretend that you also hate to watch gory, violent movies.

Now, imagine you just had a very stressful day and you want to relax and watch something on TV to take your mind off your stress. You sit down on your couch and turn on the television. In front of you is the goriest, most violent movie you have ever seen and the sound of people screaming in pain is blasting loudly. What would you do in that instance?

Chances are you would turn the TV off, change the channel, or go do something else. Would you ever sit in front of that television screen and think, "Please let this movie end. I can't stand this movie. I feel so helpless that this movie is playing in front of me. There is nothing I can do to stop this movie. I'm just a victim."

Of course, you wouldn't have these thoughts in this situation! That would be incredibly silly because you have the power to leave, turn the TV off, or change the channel. At that moment, you would take control and be the boss of that situation, wouldn't you?

What if I told you that you do, in fact, sit in front of unpleasant movies and act like a powerless victim quite often? Would it surprise you to know that you do this? Well, my dear reader, you do, in fact, do this quite often.

How often do you replay a scene of a real or perceived failure in your mind? What about recalling every single detail of an argument, or how someone once mistreated you? How many times have you replayed the movie where you were embarrassed in front of your friends or classmates? When you think about those events, how did you feel? Did you feel powerful and confident, or did you find yourself full of anxiety, fear, or self-doubt?

Remember earlier, when I said your subconscious mind is a room full of movies about you? Every time you replay an argument or beat yourself up for something that happened in the past, all you are doing is replaying that crappy movie, over and over again, and watching it as if you are powerless to change the channel. You play some movies so many times that they have found their way onto your automatic "favorite playlist."

You don't have to watch those movies or listen to the recording of them anymore. You can turn them off. Just like a television, your mind is filled with different channels. If you have an experience you don't like, be willing to change the station to something else, or turn the television off completely. I will show you how to do this when I teach you about your Inner Super Powers.

I hope by now, you are getting a lot of "Ah-Ha!" moments and things are starting to make sense for you. Let's dive into those Inner Super Powers now, so you can start taking charge of yourself and your life.

Self-Reflection

Take five minutes to think about how your life will look once you understand your Inner Super Powers and can tap into them consistently to destroy your fear and self-doubt. What would that look like? What would you do next? How would your life be different?

Go ahead and use your imagination and have fun with this self-reflection. Write down all the wonderful things you can do now because you are strong, confident, and courageous. Remember to dream big!

Free Workbook

If you don't want to write your answers down in this book, you can get a free companion workbook by visiting **JacquiLetran.com/freeworkbook**. You can print it out or complete it on your computer. (You may be able to complete the workbook on your smart phone or tablet if you have a special pdf reader.)

CHAPTER 2

The Power of Words

Words are one of our greatest and most frequently used Inner Super Powers. Words can create significant insecurities, destroy relationships, and tear families apart. Words can also have an equally positive effect. It can give a hopeless person hope, heal a broken heart, and give someone the power and courage to pursue their dreams.

You might be thinking, "wait a minute—aren't words external? How can they be an Inner Super Power?"

Great questions! Words are an Inner Super Power because your words come from within yourself. These include the words you speak out loud, of course, but more importantly, also the words you say to yourself when you think and analyze situations.

Why Words are a Super Power

Have you ever done something that you were really proud of and were really excited to share that achievement with your friends and family? However, the moment you shared your accomplishment with someone, you immediately feel deflated, embarrassed, or maybe even sad. Perhaps the words they responded with made you feel criticized. Perhaps the words they used made you feel as though you're not good enough. You might start to doubt yourself or even call yourself names. You might wonder if you are lame or even stupid for being so proud of something that no one else seemed to care about.

You are not alone in this pattern of thinking and feeling. We all have had similar negative thoughts in the back of our minds at different times that caused us to feel sad, scared, uncomfortable, or full of self-doubt. How destructive is that way of thinking?

Just a moment ago, you were feeling great. But because someone said harsh or unsupportive words to you, your happiness level plummeted. Not only did your happiness level plummet, but perhaps your self-belief and self-confidence took a dive just as quickly. Often, you will start using negative words to yourself after this type of event. Maybe you start thinking, "I'm a loser. No one cares about me or what I do."

Those silent conversations you have with yourself are exceptionally powerful because you may not even realize that they are happening. Even so, your subconscious mind is paying attention and is looking for evidence to fulfill your request to experience being a loser that no one cares about.

All of this works together to create significant negative emotions that result in you doubting yourself, your abilities, and maybe even your self-worth. That's the power of words. They can take you from total excitement and happiness to sadness, fear, and self-doubt in a flash.

The good news is that words can also have a powerfully positive effect. Imagine a time that you felt down, frustrated, isolated, and alone. Now, imagine that someone reached out to you and said just the right words—words you desperately wanted or needed to hear at that moment.

Perhaps you were feeling a lot of pain and uncertainty and a friend reached out to you and said, "You're going to be OK. I'm here for you." You went from feeling sad, alone, or frustrated to feeling a lot better almost immediately. Perhaps you might even feel safe, supported, loved, or happy. Because of these kind and supportive words, your mood changed; and it changed at the speed of thought!

You start seeing possibilities where there were only limitations before. Rather than retreating, you start looking for ways to move past this block. You feel motivated. You see solutions easily and you feel confident in your ability to solve your problems, or maybe you see a way out. This is the positive power of words!

Word Filters

Your words have immense powers. Whatever words you use to express your thoughts or feelings, whether out loud or silently to yourself, are the same words that create your reality and life experiences. In this way, it is very similar to editing a picture using a filter app.

Imagine taking a vibrant and colorful photo and putting a black and white filter on it. What would happen? Would your picture remain vibrant and colorful, or would it change into a black and white picture? If you are editing a photo using a particular filter and you don't like the result, are you going to say, "Oh, well. There's nothing I could do about it"? Or would you try out a different filter? Most likely, you would try a different filter, or at least revert back to the original picture.

Our life experiences are very similar to that. Just imagine your words are the filters, or "Word Filters," and your life experiences are the photos. Whatever Word Filters you choose to put on your life experiences will become the result you see in your "photos," which is your reality. When you have an experience you don't like, be willing to play around with different Word Filters and create the pictures that you want at that moment.

For example, let's say you tried out for a lead role in your school play and you were not chosen. The Word Filters that naturally pop up for you might sound like, "I don't deserve that part because I'm a terrible actor. Everyone else is so much better than me. Who am I kidding? I'm no good at this. Why do I even bother?" When you use these Word Filters to view your experience, how do you feel? Do you feel positive and encouraged, or do you feel sad and deflated?

Instead of allowing your old Word Filters to control your mood, what if you decided to use your Inner Super Power of Words to express yourself? What if you choose to think or say, "That actor got the role because they have three more years of experience than I do. I am a beginner and I am committed to learning and practicing so I can be my best," or "I am not the right person for this part and the right part for me will come along." When you use these Word Filters, how do you feel? Do you feel sad and deflated, or do you feel motivated to improve yourself and inspired to look for new opportunities?

The reality of the situation is that you did not get the lead role. However, how you choose to view that event will either lift you up and prepare you for the next opportunity or drag you down and discourage your ambitions. The choice is yours.

Your words are that powerful. And if you are careless with your words, you can create unwanted (and unnecessary!) pain and misery for yourself and others around you. Be purposeful in the words you use to create the experiences you want for yourself and those you care about. Choose words that are supportive, encouraging, and inspiring when you speak to yourself and others. You can create your experiences by selecting the words that empower you.

The Power of "I AM"

In the English language, the two most powerful words, when used together, are the words "I AM." Whatever you put behind "I AM" becomes your reality.

The words that immediately follow "I AM" are your declaration to your subconscious mind and the Universe: "This is who I am. Make sure I have this experience."

Let's say you are going to a party and you're feeling a little nervous. You may be worried that you will have a bad time because you believe people don't like you or that you are awkward and won't fit in. Imagine entering the party with these thoughts: "I AM going to be so uncomfortable. I AM so nervous. I AM going to feel and act so awkward."

These are your declarations and commands to your subconscious mind to make sure you have these experiences. Your subconscious mind will hear those thoughts as commands: "I want to have a bad time. Make sure I feel like I don't fit in. Make sure I feel so uncomfortable, nervous, and awkward."

Being that dedicated assistant, your subconscious mind will go to work and adjust your environment so that no matter where you look, you will get to experience the party through the Word Filters of your negative "I AM" commands.

As you sit in the corner by yourself, looking nervously around, you happen to lock eyes with someone who has an unpleasant expression on her face; maybe you see it as a disgusted expression. Immediately, you start thinking, "I KNEW IT! I shouldn't be here. Everyone thinks I'm a weirdo. What was I thinking? I'm so stupid to think I could fit in or have fun." Look what has happened—a new flood of negative commands that will reinforce your experience and your beliefs!

How damaging are your words to your confidence and self-esteem? Because you glanced up and saw someone with an unpleasant expression on her face and the Word Filters you're using are negative ones, you instantly came to a destructive conclusion that caused you to feel worse about yourself and your situation.

In reality, perhaps that girl was thinking, "I got all dressed up for Tommy and he won't even look at me. He doesn't think I'm attractive." Or maybe she's thinking, "OMG, I forgot to turn the curling iron off at home. I'm going to burn the house down! I always do stupid things like this," and the disgusted look on her face reflects her fear and her own self-judgments, which has nothing to do with you at all.

These two examples demonstrate how we are all "in our own minds," thinking about our problems. The experiences we have are of our own creation based on the words we choose when we talk to ourselves. We are all guilty of creating these negative stories in our minds. We make ourselves fearful, sad, or anxious for no reason other than because we don't feel good about ourselves in those moments and we are not fully aware of the power of our words.

How to Destroy Fear and Self-Doubt Using the Power of Words

If you feel nervous at any event or situation, you can take control by unleashing your Inner Super Power of

Words and select a different set of Word Filters. Maybe you can choose a couple of these different Word Filters instead:

"I AM OK. Everything will be OK."
"I AM willing to have fun."
"I AM calm."
"I AM excited to try something new."
"I AM courageous."
"I AM excited to meet new people."
"I AM ready to enjoy myself."

When you choose positive Word Filters like these, you begin giving your subconscious mind an entirely different set of commands. You are telling your subconscious mind to use the lenses that allow you to have positive experiences. You might even find yourself having fun and connecting with people like never before because you have actively chosen to use your Inner Super Power of Words to create meaningful experiences for yourself.

Now that you are aware of the Inner Super Power of Words, I encourage you to go through the following exercises to help you to master this power. With practice, you can easily and effectively destroy your fear and self-doubt.

Self-Reflection

1. On a scale of 0 to 10 (with 10 being the highest), how aware was I of how my words impacted myself and others prior to reading this chapter? How aware am I now?

_____

_____

_____

_____

_____

_____

_____

_____

_____

2. Here are two examples of how the words I have been using created pain for myself:

_____

_____

_____

_____

_____

_____

_____

_____

_____

_____

3. Here are two examples of how the words I have been using created pain for someone else:

_____

_____

_____

_____

_____

_____

_____

_____

_____

_____

_____

4. Here are two examples of how the words I have been using have supported, inspired, or motivated myself:

_____

_____

_____

_____

_____

_____

_____

_____

_____

_____

_____

_____

5. Here are two examples of how the words I have been using have supported, inspired, or motivated others:

_____

_____

_____

_____

_____

_____

_____

_____

_____

_____

_____

_____

6. When I do something wrong, or when something doesn't go as planned, the words I often use when talking to myself are:

_____

_____

_____

_____

_____

_____

_____

_____

_____

_____

_____

7. Now that I understand the power of my words, I am ready to choose my words wisely. Here are a few empowering words or Word Filters I can choose instead:

Example:
- I'm a beginner at ____ and that's OK."
- "Well, that didn't work out. Let's try_____ instead."
- "I know I can do better with practice."
- "I'm ready to dedicate time to achieving my goals."

_____

_____

_____

_____

_____

_____

_____

_____

_____

_____

_____

_____

_____

_____

_____

_____

_____

Tapping into the ISP of Words

Exercise One:
Inner Super Power Commands

Step 1:

Let's start by creating a few Inner Super Power Commands, or "ISP Commands," which are the Word Filters you'll use to develop and unleash your powers. To begin, after the words, "I am" below, list four traits or personality characteristics you want to create or strengthen in yourself.

For example: confident, courageous, talented, outgoing, smart, interesting, funny, attractive, positive, strong, etc.

I am _____.
I am _____.
I am _____.
I am _____.

Step 2:

Once you have created your ISP Commands, put them in a place that you can easily see them daily as a reminder to yourself of your true desire. Maybe you can write it on a post-it note and stick it on your door, or on a sheet of paper by your nightstand, or have it as your lock screen on your phone.

Step 3:

Follow this simple exercise at least twice a day with each ISP Command to create and reinforce a firm belief in them. The more times you complete this exercise, the quicker you will truly believe in your ISP Commands. Thus, the sooner you will see them reflected in your reality.

- Look directly into your eyes as you're looking in a mirror.
- Say your first ISP Command out loud with power, purpose, and determination (work on each ISP Commands individually).
- Notice how you feel emotionally and physically when you say your ISP Commands.

For example, you are working on the ISP Command, "I am smart." Look at yourself in the mirror, look directly into your eyes, and say, "I am smart." Remember to say it like you mean it.

Notice how your body responds to those words. If you feel good or neutral when saying your ISP Command, go to the next ISP Command. When you're done with all four ISP Commands and they all feel good or at least neutral, thank yourself and go on with your day. Repeat your ISP Commands several times daily.

If it doesn't feel right to say, "I am smart," then you know that you don't believe that statement currently. Be willing to dedicate a few minutes and a little effort to change that belief.

To change your beliefs effectively, here's one more detail about your subconscious mind that you should know about:

Your subconscious mind pays attention to your feelings more than the words you use.

Feelings are how your subconscious mind gauges the true meaning of your words and whether you need to be protected, or you are safe to proceed ahead.

For example, suppose you and I are best friends and I said, "Hey, ugly, what are you up to?" You probably won't think twice about the word "ugly" because that's the term of endearment we have chosen to use with each other. In fact, because it's our term of endearment, you might feel happy or connected with me when you hear that word.

If someone you don't really know or like said the same words to you, how would you feel? Chances are you would be offended, angry, or sad. Although the words are the same, the meaning and the feeling are completely different.

In the first example, your subconscious mind will look for evidence that will give you the experience of happiness and connection. In the second instance, your subconscious mind will look for evidence to support why you should be feeling offended, angry, or sad.

Remember that your subconscious mind is paying attention to your feelings to know what experience it needs to create for you.

If you say, "I am smart," and you feel anxious or notice a heaviness on your chest, then the message or command you're sending to your subconscious mind is the opposite. In this instance, it is, "I am stupid," or "I am dumb," or whatever word you would typically use to express you're not smart.

Let's pretend you typically say, "I'm an idiot," when you don't feel smart. When you say, "I am smart," and you feel that crushing pressure on your chest, the command your subconscious mind hears and will follow is, "I'm an idiot. Look for evidence to prove that I'm an idiot. I want to have the experience of feeling like an idiot." Your subconscious mind will immediately search for evidence to give you the experience of feeling like an idiot, which, of course, reinforces your beliefs.

You definitely don't want to reinforce your negative beliefs. So, when you say your ISP Command and feel any negativity, whether emotionally or physically, ease up a little with your command. You can soften it to, "I am WILLING to be _____" or even, "I am WILLING to know it's possible for me to be _____."

Softening your ISP Command will allow your subconscious mind to relax and accept your command readily because the emotion attached is different than the original strong, negative feeling.

Say the softened version of your ISP Command two to three times to get comfortable with it. Once you are comfortable or at least feeling neutral, thank yourself and go on with your day. The next time you practice your ISP Commands, go back to your "I AM" statement. You want to program your subconscious mind with the strongest commands, which are your "I AM" statements, and soften the statement ONLY if you need to.

In the rare instances when the softened version of your ISP Command still doesn't feel true, go to page 205 and follow the "Five Simple Steps to Release Your Unwanted Emotions." Using these five simple steps will allow you to release your negative emotions so you can go back to focusing on creating positive experiences for yourself.

Exercise Two: Choosing Calm

Did you know that you can learn to stay calm no matter what is happening in your environment? Imagine how incredible it would be to be able to remain calm when things are chaotic around you or falling apart. That would be a very valuable skill to have, wouldn't it? This powerful skill is very easy to learn and you can master it quickly.

Earlier, you learned that the words "I AM" are mighty words that create your reality and experiences. Whatever word(s) you put after the words "I AM" becomes your experience. To get to calm, use the power of "I AM."

The next time you have any negative feelings, get excited! This is an excellent opportunity to master the art of calmness and take control of your emotions. The process is very straightforward.

First, you want to identify your unwanted emotion. For example, you're feeling nervous.

Once you identify your emotion, say to yourself, either out loud or in your own mind, "Even though I'm (insert your emotion here), I choose to be calm. I choose to be calm. I choose to be calm. I am calm. I am calm. I am calm."

Keep repeating "I am calm," over and over until you feel calm. As you are repeating "I am calm," imagine yourself doing something that calms you down. Maybe you feel your calmest when you are laying out on the beach, or maybe it's watching YouTube videos, or listening to music. Whatever calms you down, imagine yourself doing that activity with vivid details.

Bring in as many senses as you can. See it. Touch it. Taste it. Hear it. Feel it. When you're doing this, you are basically saying to your subconscious mind, "Even though I feel (insert your emotion here), I choose to be calm. Calm looks like this. Give me this experience." When you use the Inner Super Power of Words to give your mind one simple command with vivid details, it's very easy for your mind to understand you and to deliver that experience to you quickly.

Here's another cool detail about your subconscious mind that works in your favor when you're choosing calm:

You cannot have two opposite emotions at the same time. You cannot be nervous and calm.

Whatever experience you are commanding your subconscious mind to give you, it will shift your focus and attention onto those details and give you more reasons to get into that state of mind.

This is precisely why it's hard to break out of your negative mood, too. Think of a time when you were depressed about something and your friends or family tried to cheer you up. No matter what they said or did, you couldn't seem to get out of your funk. The reason for that is because your mind can only focus on one emotion at a time and you are giving energy and commanding your subconscious mind to keep you depressed. The moment you decide to focus on something else, your subconscious mind also shifts its focus, your depression lessens, and your mood changes.

If "I AM calm" doesn't feel right, feel free to soften it up to, "I am WILLING to be calm," or even, "I am WILLING to know it's possible for me to be calm."

Now, choosing calm will work a significant amount of the time, but only if you practice using it consistently. Practice choosing calm the moment you notice any slight negative emotion that you don't want to hold on to. Minor negative emotions are easy to move away from and are great to practice with.

Every time you successfully shift your negative emotion to calm, you strengthen your ISP Command of "I am calm." Eventually, your "I am calm" command will be so strong and so automatic that it will become easy to shift to calm even when your emotions are high.

In the first chapter, *It's All in Your Mind*, you learned that you often watch those crappy movies as if you were powerless to change them. Now, you have a way to turn off those movies whenever you choose. Imagine your "*I am calm*" command is your remote control. When you choose calm, you effectively shut off the crappy movie, and instead, you get to enjoy the new movie of whatever activity you imagine as you are giving yourself the "*I am calm*" command.

Get ready to be amazed by how quickly you can turn off those old movies and take control of your emotions!

Exercise Three:
Moving from "I can't" to "I can"

Remember, everything you think and feel are commands to your subconscious mind: "This is the experience I want. Look for evidence to support why I should continue to think and feel this way."

When you say you can't do something, such as, "I can't dance," you are giving your subconscious mind the command, "Make sure I experience my inability to dance. Look for evidence to support the fact that I can't dance."

Each time you say this statement, you reinforce your beliefs and therefore, stay stuck in your inability to dance. If you want to change that and have a different experience, add the word "yet" to the end of the sentence that starts with, "I can't." Therefore, your "I can't dance" statement becomes, "I can't dance *yet*."

When you say, "I can't dance," how does that feel? Does it feel like you can take charge and change your situation and learn to dance easily?

What about the statement, "I can't dance yet?" How does that feel? It feels a lot different than "I can't dance," doesn't it? Adding "yet" to "I can't dance" tells your subconscious mind, "Even though at this moment, I'm not able to dance, my future will be different."

When you add the power of the Word Filter "yet" to any "I can't" statement, you immediately change that statement to a statement of possibilities. Adding "yet" after "I don't know how to" also works the same way. For example, "I don't know how to be comfortable in social situations yet." Adding "yet" to a statement keeps that possibility alive and makes it easier for you to pursue in the future

Let's work on changing your "I can't" into "I can." First, list your top four "I can't" or "I don't know how to" statements and add the word "yet" to the end of each statement. Notice how much differently you feel about that statement immediately.

Example:
I can't be comfortable in a large group yet.

1. _____
   _____

2. _____
   _____

3. _____
   _____

4. _____
   _____

As a bonus, you can use the statements above and create powerful ISP Commands and practice them the same way you've practiced the previous ISP Commands. For example, "I can't dance yet" can become, "I AM committed to learning how to dance" or "I AM ready to learn how to dance" or "I AM a unique dancer."

1. _____
   _____

2. _____

3. _____

4. _____

CHAPTER 3

The Power of Your Body

Your body is one of your most powerful Inner Super Powers. Your body is how you represent yourself (how you "show up" or appear) to the rest of the world.

Your body position, your facial expression, and how you move your body tells others so much about who you are. Even before people have a chance to get to know you, they will have already made a lot of assumptions about you based on your physical appearance and how you carry yourself.

When you understand the Inner Super Power of Your Body, you can show up as a warm and confident person who people are excited to meet and get to know. When I'm talking about the Inner Super Power of Your Body, I'm not talking about how you're dressed or the size of your clothes—although they could support you in feeling good about yourself. Your true power is in how you control your body.

How you move your body has the power to dramatically influence your moods; therefore, it has a significant impact on your experiences. In the past, it was commonly believed that our minds were fully responsible for controlling our body, therefore our actions. In recent years, Embodied Cognition,[1] a newer field of cognitive science (the study of the mind), emerged to show that "the mind is not only connected to the body, but that the body influences the mind." What this means is that our minds influence our bodies and our bodies influence our minds.

The findings within Embodied Cognition research is so exciting because it helps us to understand the very important roles our bodies play in influencing our moods, actions, and experiences. When you understand how simple these concepts are, you will be able to tap into the Inner Super Power of Your Body to quickly and instantly destroy your fear and self-doubt while boosting your confidence level.

In simple terms, your mind, or the thoughts and feelings you have, influences how your body reacts. Likewise, the actions and positions of your body influence how you feel, which, in turn, affects your thoughts, actions, and experiences.

Why Your Body is a Super Power

To fully understand the power of your body, let's talk about two very key concepts, the Mind's Programs and the Body's Programs.

---

[1] McNerney, Samuel. A Brief Guide to Embodied Cognition: Why You Are Not Your Brain "http://blogs.scientificamerican.com/guest-blog/a-brief-guide-to-embodied-cognition-why-you-are-not-your-brain/

The Mind's Programs

Have you ever noticed that when you're feeling an intense emotion, such as sadness, everything around you, including the small things that you typically wouldn't even notice, can cause you to feel even worse?

This is because whenever you have a certain emotion, your subconscious mind will automatically run the corresponding "mind's program" for that emotion. A mind's program can be thought of the same way as a computer program, which is a set of procedures or commands for your mind to carry out. The purpose of these emotional mind's programs is to give you—and enhance—the experience you've asked for.

In a previous chapter, you learned that your thoughts and feelings are direct commands to your subconscious mind: "This is the experience I want. Give me this experience." When you are feeling sad, you're giving your subconscious mind the command of, "I want to feel sad. Give me this experience." Your subconscious mind will immediately run your mind's program for sadness.

With the Sadness Mind's Program running, your subconscious mind will look in your movie library and find movies from your past that caused you sadness and start playing those movies in a repetitive loop. This brings those past events back into your awareness, causing you to re-experience the pain from those events again.

You stay stuck in your head, thinking about all these different painful events and your sadness persists. Perhaps you're thinking about a certain mistake you've made over and over again. Perhaps you're thinking about all the times people have rejected you and caused you pain. Or perhaps you're thinking about all the times you've let yourself or someone else down.

At the same time your old movies are playing in the background, your subconscious mind will scan your environment, looking for evidence for why you should be sad. Anything that has the potential of making you feel sad will be picked up by your subconscious mind and pointed out to you. You become hyper-aware of the things that make you sad, while the things that could make you happy get completely ignored.

Each time you play your mind's program for sadness and experience sadness, your beliefs about sadness and who you are in relation to sadness become stronger. You feel trapped within this loop, which could make you feel as though you are powerless against these repetitive thoughts. These negative, reoccurring thoughts can even lead you down a path of greater sadness and create feelings of anxiety, hopelessness, or even depression.

As if that's not bad enough, your subconscious mind will take another step to enhance the experience you've requested. Using the evidence it has picked up on from your past movies, your subconscious mind will create a new movie for you. Only, this time, it is set in the future. In this movie, you are still trapped in the repetitive patterns that caused your sadness—you're still letting yourself and others down and people are still rejecting and hurting you. This little gift from your subconscious mind helps to keep you in the experience you had asked for.

This is a very common path for the mind's program for most emotions. When you are in a particular emotional state, your subconscious mind will do everything it can to continue or heighten that feeling for you. It will replay your past movies, look for external evidence, and project similar events into your future. The net result is that you get to continue experiencing more of those same feelings.

Remember, you asked for the experience and your subconscious mind is just doing its job and being a good assistant to you.

The Body's Programs

Your body also has its own programs for your various emotions. To simplify, I will call them the "strong body program" and the "weak body program."

Typically, when you feel anxious, inferior, scared, or another similar negative emotion, your body will run the "weak body program." When the weak body program is running, you and your body tend to close up. Your shoulders might start feeling heavy or tight and your gaze might start going downward. You might start slouching, crossing your arms or legs, or even curling yourself up into the fetal position. When you feel bad about yourself or your situation, your body naturally becomes smaller, as if to hide or protect you from any real or perceived danger.

The opposite is true for when you are feeling self-assured, happy, or powerful and you are running the "strong body program." When you feel good about yourself, your body naturally opens up and your gaze is either focused ahead or upward.

A study[2] comparing blind Olympic athletes (some who were blind at birth) with athletes who can see normally shows how dramatically similarly the athletes moved their bodies in response to winning or losing an event. "The winners tilted their heads up, smiled, lifted their arms, clenched their fists and puffed out their chests, while slumped shoulders and narrowed chests were the hallmarks of losers."

Isn't that interesting? Even the athletes who were blind from birth and who have never witnessed another person's body movement would display the same body movements in response to winning or losing. The reason for this is that we are born with these automatic body programs for our feelings; these body programs are almost identical from person to person.

Think of a time when you aced a difficult test, scored the winning point for your team, or were chosen to participate in something you were really excited about. How did you react physically? Perhaps you gave your friends high-fives. Perhaps you jumped up and down or danced. Or perhaps you puffed out your chest and threw your hands up in the victory position. Every one of those actions demonstrates your body's program

---

[2] Yong, Ed. Blind Olympic athletes show the universal nature of pride and shame. http://phenomena.nationalgeographic.com/2008/08/13/blind-olympic-athletes-show-the-universal-nature-of-pride-and-shame/

for positivity and success. When you feel good about yourself, your body naturally opens up and takes up more space as if to say, "Look at me!"

Similarly, think of a time when you did something that you were really embarrassed about or ashamed of. How did your body react? Did you make direct eye contact with those around you? Did you stand there with your hands on your hips and proudly display your embarrassment or shame, or did you slink away in hopes of going unnoticed?

The Mind's and The Body's Program at Work

Let's go back to the mind's program for sadness to demonstrate how the mind's and body's programs work together. Once you've triggered the mind's program for an emotion, it runs on autopilot. Your body reacts accordingly by triggering the matching body's program.

Let's say you got into a fight with a friend and now, you're feeling sad. Your sad mind's program kicks in. You start to think about all the other times this friend has caused you pain. Your thoughts might shift to other people who have hurt you and other sad events from your past. You might even think about how this friend will hurt you again in the future.

At the same time, your body naturally responds by closing up. Your energy closes in; you cross your arms over your chest, curl yourself up in a little ball, or become listless. You might even feel mentally, emotionally, and physically drained. You don't want to do anything or talk to anyone. You just want to lie there, curled up in your misery.

All of this happens simultaneously because your mind and your body are working together, running their individual programs, to bring you the experience you've asked for, which, in this example, is sadness. Suddenly, you went from feeling a little sad to feeling very sad. If you do nothing about it and allow these programs to run, you will continue to stay sad.

Here's where it gets really exciting! Your mind and your body have to run the same program for you to continue to stay in your current emotional experience. This is really important, so let me say it again.

Your mind and your body have to run the same program for your mind to continue its path and hang onto your current emotional state.

When your mind and your body are not running the same program, your mind gets confused. When your mind gets confused, it stops running the current emotional program and your feelings change. In this way, your body is very powerful in its ability to influence your feelings.

How to Destroy Fear and Self-Doubt Using the Power of Your Body

How can you use this information to boost your confidence and destroy your fear and self-doubt?

Let's say you're feeling anxious and your mind's program for anxiety is running and causing you to think and remember more anxiety-inducing events. Your body reacts accordingly and kicks in the body's program for anxiety. You notice your body starting to close in and that you have crossed your arms. You notice that you're looking down toward the ground and you're shifting uncomfortably where you're standing.

When you notice your body closing up, what if you decided to tap into your Inner Super Power of Your Body and do something different? Instead of allowing your body to close up, what if you decided to open it up? What if you stand tall and strong, throw your arms up, look up at the sky, and smile the biggest, most confident, or even goofy smile you can imagine? How do you think you would feel if you just changed your body like that?

Let's do a quick exercise to show you what this looks like. Start by standing up with your feet hip-width distance apart. Tighten up your leg muscles and feel how strong your legs are. Stand up tall and look straight ahead and smile the biggest smile you can. Also, either place your hands on your hips or throw them up toward the sky.

How do you feel when you hold your body this way? What happens to your self-confidence level?

For the sake of this activity, go ahead and do the opposite. Start slouching your body, allow your shoulders to become heavy, cross your arms, and look down at your feet. As a bonus, go ahead and bite your lip very lightly while shuffling your feet.

How do you feel in this position? What happens to your self-confidence now? Go back and forth between these two poses and pay attention to the words you're using to yourself and how you feel differently as you move from one pose to another.

Now, imagine yourself walking into a social setting and seeing a stranger standing tall, smiling warmly, and making eye contact with you. What kind of assumptions will you make about that person solely based on how they are presenting themselves with their body? Will you see them as confident, friendly, and approachable?

Next, imagine shifting your eyes and seeing someone else sitting by herself on a bench with her head held down and her arms folded firmly across her chest. What assumptions will you make of her? Does she appear confident, friendly, or approachable?

Now, think about the people whom you thought were so lucky because they seemed confident, easygoing, and well-liked. How do they look? How do they hold their body?

To appear more confident and easygoing, all you have to do is use the Inner Super Power of Your Body. Your body affects not only how you feel about yourself, but also how others see you and the impression they make of you.

You have the power to take control and run your positive and successful body's program whenever you want to. It's as simple as the exercise you just went through. When you take on a powerful pose when you're anxious, it confuses your mind because this is not your body's program for anxiety.

Remember, when your mind and body are not running the same program, your mind gets confused. When your mind gets confused, it lets go of that current emotion. You are then free to choose a new emotion that better suits your needs at that moment.

The net result is that you get to break the cycle of feeling like a victim to your emotions and instead, reclaim your true power at the moment.

The next time you go into a situation that causes you fear or self-doubt, use the Inner Super Power of Your Body. Instead of slouching in your chair, looking down at the table, and wringing your hands as you're sitting in class, anxiously waiting for your turn to give your presentation, sit up straight.

Use the Inner Super Power of Your Body to relax your shoulders and allow them to drop comfortably. Uncross your legs, turn your knees outward, and plant your feet firmly on the ground. Look directly ahead of you or at the line where the wall and ceiling meet.

The simple act of focusing your energy and attention on keeping your body open and strong will break your negative emotional state, and help you to look and feel a sense of confidence instantly. You can then choose the Word Filters you want to create the experience you're looking for.

Self-Reflection

1. When I am nervous, scared, or tense, how does my body naturally react?

_____

_____

_____

_____

_____

_____

_____

_____

_____

2. When I feel good about something I've just done or about myself, how does my body naturally react?

_____

_____

_____

_____

_____

_____

_____

_____

_____

_____

3. Here are two specific examples where my body closed up and caused me to feel even worse about my situation:

_____

_____

_____

_____

_____

_____

_____

_____

_____

_____

_____

_____

_____

_____

_____

_____

_____

_____

_____

_____

_____

_____

_____

_____

4. Here are two specific examples where my body opened up and caused me to feel good about my situation:

_____

_____

_____

_____

_____

_____

_____

_____

_____

_____

_____

_____

_____

_____

_____

_____

_____

_____

_____

_____

_____

_____

_____

_____

5. Think about the people you admire. How do they hold their body in stressful situations? What could you learn from them?

_____

_____

_____

_____

_____

_____

_____

_____

_____

_____

6. Think about the people you admire. How do they look that tells you they are comfortable with themselves? What could you learn from them?

_____

_____

_____

_____

_____

_____

_____

_____

_____

Tapping into the ISP of Your Body

Exercise One: Physical Movements

Engaging in physical activities on a regular basis is a great way for you to feel better. When you participate in physical activities, not only are you tapping into the Inner Super Power of Your Body, you are also releasing endorphins, the feel-good hormone that lifts you up.

For some people, physical activities might be difficult or painful, making this exercise a little more challenging. However, even with this constraint, challenge yourself to look for activities that you could comfortably participate in, even if it's only for a short duration.

1. What type of physical activities do I enjoy?

_____

_____

_____

_____

_____

_____

_____

_____

_____

_____

2. Pick one or two of the above activities from the list above and dedicate thirty minutes to each activity at least once a week. Pay close attention to how you feel during and after your activities and write your thoughts below. (**NOTE:** If you have constraint that makes physical activities difficult, feel free to adjust the time to match your current ability. Remember this is not an "all or nothing" activity. If you can only engage for two minutes at first, that's perfectly fine. Keep it up and you'll soon be able to extend this time.)

3. Instead of allowing my body to close up when I don't feel good, I could choose to do these activities: (Examples: brisk walking, jumping jacks, push-ups, sitting up straight, relax my shoulders, gaze forward).
(**NOTE:** Think of simple activities that you can do almost anywhere and require no special planning or equipment.)

_____

_____

_____

_____

_____

_____

_____

_____

_____

_____

_____

_____

_____

Exercise Two: Mastering the Moves

1. Watch a few YouTube videos of your favorite sports and pay close attention to how the athletes enter the field or arena. How did they appear? How did they move their body? Watch what happens when they or their teammate score a point or win a game. How did they react? What did they do with their body? Write down what you've observed. (**NOTE:** If you don't like sports, look for other competitions to watch and pay attention to how the competitors respond when they win.)

_____

_____

_____

_____

_____

_____

_____

_____

_____

_____

_____

_____

_____

_____

_____

_____

_____

2. Next, mimic the athletes or competitors body movements. If they jumped, you jump. If they high-fived someone, high-five someone. If there is no one around you, high-five yourself, or imagine high-fiving your best friend. If they threw their hands up in a victory position, do the same. How did you feel when you engaged in these body movements? Did you notice your confidence level or energy rising? Write your experiences down.

_____

_____

_____

_____

_____

_____

_____

_____

_____

_____

_____

_____

_____

_____

_____

_____

_____

_____

_____

_____

Exercise Three: Power Pose

Read about the four Power Poses below and choose one Power Pose to practice daily for two minutes. As an alternative, you can also mimic one of the power moves you've witnessed from watching your favorite athletes in action after they've just won a game or tournament.

Power Pose One:
Stand with your feet hip-width distance apart. Plant your feet firmly on the ground. Imagine there are roots coming from the bottom of your feet, anchoring you to the ground and giving you extra support. Tighten up your leg muscles and notice how strong they are. Throw your arms up in the air and make fists with your hands. Tighten up your arm muscles and notice how strong they are. Look straight ahead or toward the sky and smile widely. You can choose to hold this position or pump your arms up and down if you like.

Power Pose Two:
Stand in the exact position as mentioned above. Instead of throwing your arms up in the air, place them on your hips. Look straight ahead or toward the sky and smile widely.

Power Pose Three:
Sit down on a comfortable chair. Put your feet up on a coffee table (or something that is at least that tall or taller) and lean back. Clasp your hands behind your

head, look straight ahead or toward the sky and smile widely. (**NOTE:** Make sure it's OK with your parents that you put your feet up on the furniture. If this is not acceptable in your house, get a tall paper box. It works beautifully.)

Power Pose Four:
Sit down on a comfortable chair. Plant your feet hip-width distance apart and rotate your knees outward. Place your hands on your upper thigh with your palms facing upward. Sit up straight and look ahead or toward the sky and smile widely.

Why do these Power Poses work?
Social Psychologist Amy Cuddy's research[3] on body language shows that when you take a "Power Pose" (which is any body position that is strong, powerful, and confident) and hold that pose for two minutes daily, you can increase the level of testosterone while decreasing the levels of cortisol in your blood stream.

Why is this important?

Your level of testosterone increases your feeling of power and dominance, which increases your confidence and self-assurance. Cortisol is your stress hormone. When your cortisol level is high, you feel more stress. Likewise, when your cortisol level is low, you feel less stressed.

---

[3] Cuddy, Amy. (2012) Your body language may shape who you are. https://www.ted.com/talks/amy_cuddy_your_body_language_shapes_who _you_are

Isn't is powerful that in just two minutes a day, you can train your mind to release the hormones that help you to be more confident while lowering your stress?

CHAPTER 4

The Power of Imagination

F or a moment, think about an early childhood
   memory when you spent numerous hours playing
   with your imaginary best friend, having fun in
your imaginary land, and doing exactly what you
wanted to do.

If you didn't have an imaginary friend, think of a
time when you were reading a great book and got
completely lost in a make-believe land or immersed in
the adventures you were reading about. Or maybe think
of a time when you were sick in bed and instead of
being bored, you used your imagination and turned
your bedroom into a jungle gym or a space station
ready to blast into outer space!

Stop reading this book for a few minutes; as vividly
as you can, bring back one or more memories of a fun
childhood experience. Take your time doing this
exercise so you can get the full experience of this next
Inner Super Power.

Now, check in with yourself. As you imagine these
events from your past, how do you feel? How is your

body positioned? If you took the time to vividly recall one of those wonderful memories, chances are you're feeling a little light-hearted, the fun memories are bringing a smile to your face, and your body is naturally open.

You might not have known it when you were younger, but in those moments, you were using your Inner Super Power of Imagination to create your own amusement and entertain yourself. You were also using your Inner Super Power of Imagination to recall those wonderful memories just now.

Why Imagination is a Super Power

Imagination helps you to entertain yourself, but what is imagination exactly, and what else is imagination good for?

Imagination[4] is defined as "the act or power of forming a mental image of something not present to the senses or never before wholly perceived in reality." It is also defined as, "the ability to confront and deal with a problem," and "a creation of the mind."

Based on these definitions, you can see why Imagination is an Inner Super Power. With your imagination, you have the ability to create mental images of something that doesn't even exist in reality—something no one may have ever seen or even thought of before!

---

[4] "imagination." Merriam-Webster.com. 2017.
https://www.merriam-webster.com (7 November 2017).

With your imagination, you can create endless journeys and adventures that entertain you and bring you excitement and happiness. Imagination gives you the ability to look at different angles of problems and come up with alternative solutions that satisfy you. When you tap into your Inner Super Power of Imagination, you have the ability to fill your life with fun activities that bring you joy and creative solutions that can fill you with a sense of adventure or accomplishment.

You use your imagination all day long, yet you probably haven't thought much about how incredible your imagination is. You might even downplay the powers of your imagination by saying, "I don't have a good imagination," or "It's only in my imagination."

Let's explore those two common statements a bit. There are a lot of people who think they don't have a good imagination. Because they believe this about themselves, they are, in fact, giving their subconscious mind the command: "Make sure to look for evidence that I'm not imaginative." Being your loyal assistant, your subconscious mind kicks-in to give you that experience, as you've requested.

The fact is that you were born with this precious gift and you do have a great imagination. If you didn't have a good imagination, you wouldn't be able to recall past events in your mind. It's with your imagination that you're able to "see" your friend's face, or feel their warm embrace long after you have parted ways. It's your imagination that you use to help you decide how to solve fun things, such as puzzles or games, to more serious things such as how to patch things up after you've hurt someone.

You have been using your imagination and the power of your mind all along. You just didn't know how powerful your imagination really is, nor how to use it consistently to create the results you want. But that's about to change.

How to Destroy Fear and Self-Doubt Using the Power of Your Imagination

Did you know that it is entirely possible to destroy your fear and self-doubt by tapping into the Inner Super Power of Imagination? From her studies[5], Dr. Stephanie Carlson, a prominent scientist who specializes in researching how our brains work, determined that with repetition, you can become the person you pretend to be.

What this means is that if you want to be confident, you can become confident by pretending to be confident. To pretend, you have to use your Inner Super Power of Imagination.

Remember, one definition of imagination is, "forming a mental image of something not present or never before wholly perceived in reality." So, when you imagine yourself confident, you are just forming a

---

[5] Carlson, Stephanie M. et al Evidence for a relation between executive function and pretense representation in preschool children. (2014)
https://www.ncbi.nlm.nih.gov/pmc/articles/PMC3864685/

mental image of yourself in a way that you haven't been before (or haven't consistently been before.)

Think of all the amazing things in your life that you enjoy so much, such as your smartphone, a game console, or even your favorite shoes. For those things to come into reality for you to enjoy, someone had to first imagine them. And not only does someone have to imagine them, but they also have to imagine them in a positive way, a way that brings excitement into that project. Without imagination, nothing would ever get created.

It is no different for you. If you want to be a certain way, you can use your imagination to bring that version of yourself to life. You can use the power of your imagination to see yourself as a fully confident version of yourself.

How do you look? What are you saying? Who are you with? What are you doing? You can use your imagination to vividly see yourself going after what you want with confidence and achieving your goals with ease. Notice how good it feels to just imagine that possibility.

Here's another fun detail about your subconscious mind that helps you bring the things you imagine into real life:

Your subconscious mind doesn't know the difference between real or imagined events.

To your subconscious mind, your real or imagined events are just programs. As a program, it's either on or off. So, if you're thinking it, feeling it, or doing something, your subconscious mind will view it as a current event that is happening in that moment.

So, when you vividly imagine yourself tackling a problem with confidence over and over again, your subconscious mind will believe that you have been successful at tackling that problem with confidence many times. If you have been successful in overcoming a problem ten or twenty times, will you still have the fear or self-doubt the next time you face that problem?

Not likely.

However, if there is still some doubt, you can change that by imagining the successful completion of that task easily and with confidence another twenty—or hundred—times.

Here's another fact about your subconscious mind that is important to create your desired outcome. In an earlier chapter, you learned that your subconscious mind is very literal and will obey your command in the easiest, quickest way possible. When you use the power of your imagination, be sure to use present-tense terms.

This looks like: "I am confident in who I am," instead of "Once I'm confident in who I am, I will..."

When you say and imagine, "I am confident in who I am," you bring your goals of being confident into the present moment. Your subconscious mind will hear and obey the command: "I am confident now. Give me the experience of being confident now."

When you say, "Once I'm confident in who I am, I will..." you're telling your subconscious mind, "Give me the experience of being confident... someday. I want to be confident at some point in the future."

You might say, "I am OK with being confident someday. It doesn't have to be today." While that's fine to feel that way, imagine what it would be like to take control and change that now.

Besides, your subconscious mind will need you to give this command consistently to rewrite your old programming. Now is the perfect time to take those first steps in making your permanent change.

Am I a Fraud?

I'm sure you have heard the expression, "Fake it till you make it." There's a lot of truth to that statement according to Dr. Stephanie Carlson's research[6]. However, to many people, the idea of faking something or pretending to be someone they're not feels dishonest and wrong.

Many times, I've heard clients say, "I don't want to lie to myself. That is just not right." Or, "I feel silly pretending to be someone I'm not." When you fake it till you make it, you can look at it as "pretending, lying, or deceiving," or you can look at it as "practicing."

When you go to the gym and work out with weights, are you tricking your body into developing muscles? Of course, you're not! You are actively participating in

---

[6] Carlson, Stephanie M. et al Evidence for a relation between executive function and pretense representation in preschool children. (2014)
https://www.ncbi.nlm.nih.gov/pmc/articles/PMC3864685/

activities that result in your muscles being developed. You are, in fact, practicing with weights to strengthen and build your physical muscles.

Imagination is a mental muscle. Instead of thinking of it as tricking yourself or lying to yourself, how about changing those Word Filters to "practicing," "strengthening," or "developing" your mental muscles? Doesn't it feel good when you choose to actively engage in developing your physical muscles?

Choose to look at your mental muscles the same way and allow yourself to feel good each time you practice this new skill. With repetition, your beliefs become stronger and more developed and your brain chemistry changes to match.

Your Personal Creation Studio

Here's a really fun way to view your imagination. Think of your imagination as your Personal Creation Studio, or "Studio" for short. Your Studio is your private playground, a place that is safe for you to test out and practice anything you want to develop, whether that's a skill or a thing you want to create.

If you want to develop a certain trait or create a new thing, you can go into your Studio and try out different ways of bringing that goal to life. The cool thing about your Studio is that it's your own private place where you are free to try and try again until you're happy with your result.

In your Studio, there is no pressure; there is no judgment. If you arrive at a result you don't like, you can adjust different aspects of it, or you can scrap it altogether. Your Studio is equipped with the "do-over" button and you can use that as many times as you want. You have full control of what goes on here!

Let's say you have a fear of talking in front of a group of people and you want to change that. You can start by going to your Studio and practicing visualizing yourself walking up to a group of people, smiling, and saying "hi." Imagine the people you've just approached smiling and saying "hi" back. Do that a few times to feel more comfortable.

Next, imagine yourself standing in a group and being fully present. This means while you're in a group setting, you're not in your head, trying to come up with things to say. Rather, you are there, listening to the conversation and enjoying the moment.

Next, imagine yourself adding to the conversation and imagine the people responding back positively. If you imagine these scenarios over and over again and you feel good when you imagine them, how do you think you'll be different in a real social setting?

Here's a hint that will help you be successful in social situations:

> When you are actively listening to a conversation, it is much easier to have something to say because you are hearing what is being said and can respond appropriately.

When you're in your head, thinking about what to say, it feels forced and unnatural. By the time you come up with something to say, the conversation has already moved on and what you came up with may no longer be appropriate, making you look or feel awkward.

Remember, your subconscious mind doesn't know the difference between real or imagined events. If you're in your head, thinking about being laughed at for saying the wrong thing, your subconscious mind will think you just, in fact, had that experience.

Similarly, if you took the time to imagine yourself at ease and having fun in a social situation twenty times, your subconscious mind would believe that you had fun in a social situation twenty times—twenty actual events where you were at ease and confident while hanging out with others.

When you actually interact with a group the first time in real life, your subconscious mind will think this is the twenty-first time that you've interacted in a group. Since the first twenty times were so wonderful, your subconscious mind has no reason to "protect" you with fear or doubt. Thus, you get to relax and enjoy your time.

With each time you imagine yourself successful, you strengthen your mental muscles and build up the skills necessary for you to be comfortable in a social setting. The best part is you did that all in your Studio, where there are no risks, only opportunities to practice!

The problem is that many people don't understand the enormous power of imagination. Rather than using their Studio to empower themselves, they use it to practice being someone they don't want to be and create scenarios that are damaging to their emotional and physical health.

Before they go into a social situation, they would imagine going to a party where everyone knows each other and they are the only one who doesn't know anyone. Or they might imagine themselves being the only one who is nervous and awkwardly saying the wrong things and being laughed at or ignored.

This, of course, further increases their fear, anxiety, and self-doubt. By the time they get into that social situation, their anxiety level is so high that they do, in fact, look and act awkward. Their body closes in, they shift uncomfortably, and they can't make eye contact with people.

Similarly, some people spend so much time in their Studio reliving past painful events that it causes them to experience physical symptoms of stress. This interferes with their sleep, their ability to focus, and decreases the over all quality of their lives. They created all of this because they didn't understand the power of their imagination. Anytime you catch yourself creating unwelcomed situations in your Studio, know that you have the power to stop that now.

Remember, your subconscious mind is always paying attention to your commands. When you think or feel a certain way (and you do this using your imagination), your subconscious mind will do all it can to give you the experience you're creating in your Studio.

Your imagination has a very important and vital role in helping you solve problems and be happy. When you actively engage your Inner Super Power of Imagination and use your Studio to practice being the person you want to be, you will change how you feel about yourself and how you feel about your world. You will be able to see problems from different angles and come up with new ways to approach and solve those problems.

Here's a key point to remember:

In every situation, you have to focus your energy and attention on something, whether that's a negative, neutral, or positive aspect of that event. Your mind cannot be completely blank. Why not choose to focus your attention on something that will make life easier and more fun for yourself?

Self-Reflection

1. Think of the last time you actively engaged the power of your Imagination, whether by watching a movie, reading a book, or just creating something great in your mind. How did you feel?

_____
_____
_____
_____
_____
_____
_____
_____
_____
_____
_____

2. Think of a time where you allowed the power of your Imagination to get the best of you and became fearful or full of self-doubt. What were you imagining? How did you feel?

_____
_____
_____
_____
_____
_____
_____
_____
_____
_____
_____

3. Go into your Studio and come up with two different ways you can think about the situation you just mentioned. Remember to engage your Inner Super Powers of Word and Your Body along with your Imagination to create new, powerful scenarios. Have fun in your Studio. Your new scenarios could involve fairies, werewolves, unicorns, and super heroes if you like. Remember, this is your private playground. Have fun and tap into your imagination. How do you feel now, having imagined the situation in a different and positive light?

_____

_____

_____

_____

_____

_____

_____

_____

_____

_____

_____

_____

_____

_____

_____

_____

_____

_____

_____

_____

_____

_____

_____

_____

Tapping into the ISP of Imagination

Exercise One: Story Time

Everyone loves a good story, whether the story is in the form of a book, a movie, a music video, or a picture collage. Stories allow you to connect to your imagination on a much deeper level because when you are involved in a story, you tend to let go of the distractions around you. Without the distractions, your imagination is free to explore endless possibilities.

1. Grab a book or a short story you've been wanting to read and start reading. Pay close attention to how you feel as you are going on the adventures with the main character. Notice how simple words on a piece of paper can cause your imagination to go wild and bring on a variety of feelings. Record what you notice below.

_____

_____

_____

_____

_____

_____

_____

_____

_____

_____

_____

_____

_____

Exercise Two: Creation Time

Let's head back into your Studio and spend a little time thinking about a story you want to tell. Using the spaces provided below or on a separate piece of paper, write down all the important details.

Who are the main characters? What are they doing? How do they look physically? How are they dressed? What are their thoughts and feelings? What is this story about? Are there any challenges your characters have to overcome?

Once you have the important details created, go ahead and tell your story. You might write a short story, a poem, or a song. Maybe you want to create a comic strip, a dance, or shadow puppet routine. Maybe you want to create a collage, a video, or a painting.

Regardless of which medium you use to tell your story, use your imagination to make it come alive. Notice how amazing your imagination is as you spend some time strengthening your sense of imagination and having fun.

_____

_____

_____

_____

_____

_____

_____

_____

_____

_____

_____

_____

Exercise Three: ISP Commands 2.0

Go back to the ISP Commands you've created from chapter two and let's make them stronger. Here are the steps:

Step 1: Below, rewrite each ISP Command.

_____

_____

_____

_____

_____

_____

_____

_____

_____

_____

Step 2: For each ISP Command, imagine yourself successfully being that way. What does that look like? How do you look, feel, and act? How do you choose to respond to people? How do they respond to you? What else do you notice? Write the details down as if it's a mini-movie script.

Example:
Step 1: I am confident.
Step 2: I feel good about myself. I know that I am funny and creative. I am relaxed and comfortable. I say what I want to say and do what I want to do. I am accepted as I am. People like being around me because

I put them at ease. I am proud of my accomplishments and I love being who I am.

_____

_____

_____

_____

_____

_____

_____

_____

_____

_____

_____

_____

_____

_____

_____

_____

_____

_____

_____

_____

_____

_____

_____

_____

_____

_____

_____

_____

_____

Step 3: Twice daily, practice your ISP Command by looking directly at yourself as you say your ISP Command with power and purpose. Then, close your eyes and bring that scene you just wrote to life. Use your Imagination to create vivid details and enjoy yourself!

CHAPTER 5

The Power of Courage

When you think of the word "courage" and someone who is courageous, what comes to mind? Who comes to mind? Do you envision someone jumping out of an airplane into enemy territories in the middle of the night? Do you imagine someone scaling a towering, icy mountain or scuba diving with sharks hundreds of feet below? Do you think of someone standing up against a group of hostile people, pushing back and fighting for social change or human justice?

For many, this is how they view courage. To be courageous, many think they must accomplish a nearly impossible task filled with risks of personal injury or even death. After all, it's these epic events that get celebrated in the media and talked about non-stop around the dinner table or among a group of friends.

When compared to these courageous heroes, many people feel bad about themselves because they have trouble thinking about getting out of bed and facing the day, let alone taking those type of enormous risks. Too many people get trapped in this way of thinking, which causes self-doubt, fear, and negative self-judgment.

Maybe you are caught in this pattern, too, and you don't know how to stop feeling bad about yourself or your situation. Once you understand true courage and how to tap into your Inner Super Power of Courage, how you view yourself and what you are capable of will dramatically change for the better.

Why Courage is a Super Power

Courage[7] is defined as "the ability to do something that frightens one" and "the mental or moral strength to venture, persevere, and withstand danger, fear, or difficulty."

Simply put, courage is the strength and ability to face something that YOU see as frightening, difficult, or dangerous. To be courageous, you do not need to climb Mount Everest, tame wild beasts, or stand up against a firing squad. To be courageous, you only need to stand up and face the things YOU are afraid of and find difficult.

Based on these definitions, you are courageous. You are much more courageous than you've realized and much more courageous than you've given yourself credit for. In the words of Nobel Peace Prize winner

---

[7] "courage." Merriam-Webster.com. 2017. https://www.merriam-webster.com (7 November 2017).

Nelson Mandela, "I learned that courage was not the absence of fear, but the triumph over it.[8]"

Think about that statement and then think about the count-less times you took a step toward something that completely frightened YOU.

How about that time you were finally able to strike up a conversation with someone you found intimidating? Maybe your heart pounded rapidly and you stumbled on your words, but you did it. And even if the results may not have been what you wanted, the fact is that you found the courage to face your fear at that moment.

What about the time you stood your ground and said what you wanted to say? Yes, it was scary, and perhaps you might have even second-guessed yourself for speaking your mind, but the fact is you did. You courageously did it! You looked directly at your fear and decided to go for it! This, in and of itself, is an incredible act of courage that went unnoticed by the world around you—and it probably even went unnoticed by you.

You have been courageous so many times in your life, but you just haven't given yourself the proper credit and acknowledgment. You don't have to let these incredibly courageous moments go unnoticed anymore. You can recognize them, choose to celebrate them, and in doing so, increase your connection to your courage and how often you engage this Inner Super Power throughout your day.

8

https://www.brainyquote.com/quotes/quotes/n/nelsonmand178789.html

Each tiny, seemingly insignificant act of courage you undertake strengthens your self-belief and stretches the boundaries of who you are a little more. When you start to notice and celebrate these wins, however small they might be, you feel good about yourself.

Remember, your subconscious mind is always paying attention to your thoughts and feelings to know what type of experiences you are looking for. When you celebrate these wins, your mind has to take notice. It will look for more evidence to show you just how courageous and capable you really are.

You feel more self-assured. You begin to see yourself differently. You start to think and act differently. You allow yourself to take more chances and do the things you want to do because you trust yourself more.

The courage and confidence that grow out of these seemingly unimportant events begin to take shape. You become more and more comfortable challenging yourself and pushing yourself to achieve even more. The things you once thought were big road-blocks become possible and your goals for even greater success are now within reach.

Courage opens up your world; the possibilities are endless. True courage is acting when you feel fear and it is also listening to and following your heart. Courage is accepting yourself exactly as you are. Courage allows you to push through when life gets tough. Courage allows you to connect to others in a deep and meaningful way.

It takes courage—lots of it—to allow others to see your vulnerabilities, your scars, and your quirks. It takes courage to dream big and pursue that dream until it becomes a reality. It takes courage to move on from situations or people that are toxic and unhealthy for you.

When you tap into your Inner Super Power of Courage and face your fear, you become unstoppable.

How to Destroy Fear and Self-Doubt Using the Power of Courage

Many people have so much fear and self-doubt that they can't relax and be themselves. They work hard to avoid the people and situations they are frightened of. They are always on high alert, watching their environment, looking for danger. They continuously try to be the person they think others want them to be. This constant need to be vigilant about their situation and the self-imposed need to figure out who they need to be in each moment amplifies their fear and self-doubt.

Imagine having to guess what each person expects from you and then trying to act in such a way to meet their expectations with every interaction you have. How exhausting would that be?

With each person you try to impress, you pretend to be the person you think they want you to be and you lose a little more of yourself. Soon, you lose connection to who you really are and the beauty and uniqueness that is you begins to fade away. This leaves you even more confused about who you are. How can you be confident and courageous when you don't even know who you are and what you stand for?

The same goes for always being on guard for potential situations that could bring you pain or disappointment. Imagine not being able to relax in any situation because you are continually looking for your escape route. Instead of being present and enjoying each moment, you stay trapped inside your head, thinking of all the things that could go wrong so you could "prepare" yourself. The harder you try to control your environment and those around you, the less you feel comfort-able in your own skin and the more fear and self-doubt you'll create.

When you practice acts of courage, you can eliminate the need to control your environment and the need to change yourself to please others. Courage will allow you to be yourself and to be genuinely comfortable in your own skin.

Here's a little fact you may not know about that will instantly help you to live more courageously:

Fear exists only in your imagination. Fear is created by recalling events from the past or imagining events in the future. Fear does not always exist in the present moment.

Therefore, if you turn all of your attention on being in the present moment, you instantly eliminate your fear.

"Wait!" you say. "I'm always afraid. Fear is with me every moment, even in the present moment!"

Let's look at those statements a bit to see if they are really true. First, think of the last time you were fearful. What kind of thoughts was running through your mind? Let's pretend that you had a class presentation and you were afraid. You probably had some, if not all, of these thoughts:

1. I'm going to be so nervous.
2. I'm going to forget what I need to say.
3. I'm going to make a fool of myself.
4. People will laugh at me.
5. I will get a bad grade.
6. I'm terrible at public speaking.
7. I've made a fool of myself in the past.
8. I'm just too scared.

Let's look at the first five statements. All of these statements are based in the future. These are things you are afraid of and you're hoping to avoid them in your future.

Statements six and seven are based on your past experiences. You believe you are a terrible public speaker because of how you presented in the past and you view that event as you making a fool of yourself.

You might say that statement eight is based on the present moment and you are somewhat correct. "I AM" is a present-tense statement; however, when you go deeper and ask, "why are you scared?" the answer will either be based on a future event ("I'm scared because I might fail.") or based on your past experiences ("I'm scared because I've done poorly in the past.").

Instead of letting your past experiences and fear of the future control your reactions, what if you tapped into your Inner Super Power of Courage to stay in the present? It takes courage to let go of old familiar patterns and start down a new, unknown path. As you're sitting in your chair, waiting for your turn to present, instead of entertaining those old fearful thoughts, what if you just focused on the moment? Maybe your classmate, Amie, is giving her presentation and you focus all of your attention on what she's saying. Maybe Amie is wearing a shirt with a really cool pattern and you spend your time mentally tracing the outline of that pattern.

Maybe you can spend your time taking slow, deliberate breaths and focusing on your Inner Super Power of Words to boost yourself up, or opening up your body to stay calm and confident. Maybe you use your Inner Super Power of Imagination and mentally practice delivering your presentation with confidence. When you courageously decide to stop the old chatter in your mind and do something positive for yourself, the outcome will be drastically improved.

Remember, having courage does not mean that you have no fear. Rather, it means looking at your fears and taking actions to overcome them. The best way to strengthen your Inner Super Power of Courage is by doing something courageous.

It might seem very counter-intuitive to say, "I don't have the courage to do the things I want to do, but I'm going to do it anyway because I want to be courageous."

You might be thinking, "That's easy for you to say because you don't have my problem. You don't know what it's like to be me and live with my fear. You don't know how much I've already suffered."

While it is completely true that I do not know your unique circumstances, I do know that we all struggle with our own challenges, fear, and self-doubt. I also know that courage is a skill that you can learn to master with patience and practice. I'm not suggesting that you take your biggest fear and tackle it head-on. That method might backfire and reinforce your belief that your fear is justified and impossible to overcome.

Courage is another mental muscle. It gets better with constant use. To start exercising your muscle for courage, start small and build your courage muscles up along the way. Find little ways to push yourself or expose yourself to new things every day. It might feel a bit awkward at first to do something outside of your comfort zone. The more you continue to push past your comfort zone, the more your comfort zone will expand.

Let's say that singing is a passion of yours, and something that you're really good at. You may want to pursue this as a career, but the idea of performing in front of others terrifies you. What small steps could you take to overcome your fear?

Perhaps the first step is singing a few songs to your family. Perhaps it's singing to a group of your close friends. For some, it's easier to do the thing they are afraid of with people they don't know. If this is you, maybe you can look for opportunities to sing to a small group of strangers. Could you look for opportunities to sing at a daycare or a nursing home? Gradually increase the size of the group and the duration of your performance until you feel at ease performing for an audience.

Remember, you can practice and perfect all of your courageous acts within the safety of your Studio before doing it in real life.

With continued practice, courageous acts will become second nature to you and your confidence will become more and more obvious in the way you live.

Self-Reflection

1. Think of three different times where you were acting courageous, but did not give yourself the proper credit. Write down all the relevant details.

_____

_____

_____

_____

_____

_____

_____

_____

_____

_____

_____

_____

_____

_____

_____

_____

_____

_____

_____

_____

_____

_____

_____

_____

_____

2. As you consider the events you wrote about in question one through the lens of courage, how did it make you feel differently?

_____

_____

_____

_____

_____

_____

_____

_____

_____

_____

_____

_____

3. Think about each event again individually. For each event, is there something you wished you would have done or said differently? Write those things down.

_____

_____

_____

_____

_____

_____

_____

_____

_____

_____

_____

_____

_____

_____

_____

_____

_____

_____

_____

_____

_____

_____

_____

_____

_____

_____

_____

_____

_____

_____

_____

_____

_____

_____

_____

4. Next, pick one of those events to practice with. Imagine going into your Studio and reacting the same way you wish you had. Practice this way of being over and over again until it feels comfortable to you. This exercise will help you to react in this way in your future. Feel free to practice reacting the way you want with the other events, too.

Tapping into the ISP of Courage

Exercise One: Small Acts of Courage

Spend the next ten minutes thinking about what you have been wanting to try. This could be anything from a new food to a new hairstyle. Create a list of things you could do to challenge yourself and work up your courage. Keep this list challenging, yet LIGHT. We'll deal with the bigger challenges later.

Here are a few examples: strike up a conversation with somebody new, experiment with different accessories, try a new recipe, sign up for a class that you've been thinking about, learn a new language or a few phrases, go to the movies by yourself, etc.

Courage is also making that decision to stop doing something that makes you uncomfortable or unhappy. For example, "stop being friends with people who constantly put me down or make fun of me," or "stop eating junk food when I'm stressed out," or "stop saying 'yes' to things I don't want to do."

As you come up with new ideas, keep adding to this list.

_____

_____

_____

_____

_____

_____

Exercise Two: Big Acts of Courage

1. Spend the next ten to fifteen minutes examining your life. What areas would you like to improve? What has been holding you back? How can you take charge and make your life more meaningful for you? Make a list of goals you would like to achieve. Think big here. Look for situations which you find difficult, challenging, or scary.

Below, create a list of three to five goals you would like to accomplish within the next three months.

_____

_____

_____

_____

_____

_____

_____

_____

_____

_____

_____

_____

_____

_____

_____

_____

_____

_____

_____

_____

_____

2. Now, look at your goals and reorder them from the easiest to the most difficult for you. Next, pick out one of your easier goals to start working on.

_____

_____

_____

_____

_____

_____

_____

_____

_____

_____

_____

_____

_____

_____

_____

_____

_____

_____

_____

_____

_____

_____

_____

_____

_____

3. Decide what date you want to accomplish your goal by and create a plan for achieving that goal. Next, come up with three to five actions you're choosing to take to accomplish your goal. For example, let's say one of your goals is to be on your school's tennis team and you are terrified of the try-out that is happening in two months. However, you are ready to take steps toward achieving this goal. Your goal could look something like:

Goal and Timeline: I am ready, comfortable, and excited for tennis try-out in two months (write the actual date here).

Action Steps:
1. Sign up for private tennis lessons this week
2. Attend and participate in every tennis class
3. Practice serving three times a week for thirty minutes
4. Play tennis with a tennis buddy twice a week for an hour
5. Practice ISP Command: "I am an awesome tennis player," while standing in Power Pose #2 twice daily

When you give yourself a timeline and create action steps like this, it will give you and your mind a very concrete plan to follow. This allows you to see exactly what you need to do to accomplish your goal and make it easier for you.

You can also engage your Inner Super Power of Imagination and train your mind to stay calm, focused, and relaxed during your try out. Start by vividly imagining yourself already achieving your goal at the try-out. See yourself playing your best game ever and feel how excited and proud you are of your skills. Imagine your coach nodding at you in approval and cheering you on.

As you vividly imagine this scenario, bring in as many senses as you can. See the game, feel your pride, hear the crowd cheer for you, taste your sweat, etc. The more vivid the details are in your mind, the easier it is for your mind to bring this into your reality. Do this exercise several times each day and get ready to be amazed at how calm you'll be when it's time to take action.

Here's another example for courageously achieving your goals using your Inner Super Powers of Words, Body, Imagination, and Courage.

Goal and Timeline: In two months, I am comfortable talking freely when I'm in a group setting.

Action Steps:
1. Create two ISP Commands for my goal and practice them twice a day: "I am comfortable talking freely when I'm in a group setting," and "I am fully present when I'm with people."
2. Practice Power Pose #1 for two minutes each day. If I find myself nervous, I can easily shift into that body position and boost my confidence.

3. Practice being present. When I feel nervous, I will take several deep breaths and focus my attention back on to the conversation.

4. Go to my Studio and practice using my imagination to visualize the following scenario twice daily. "I am calm, comfortable, and relaxed as I stand around, talking to a group of people. I breathe normally. My heart beats normally. I am focused on the conversation and on enjoying myself. I speak freely. It feels good to be in a group setting and enjoying myself."

5. After two weeks of practicing visualizing the scenario in my Studio, I will find two people to talk to and practice staying comfortable while talking in real life. At first, that could be a three or four-minute conversation. Every two weeks, I will expand my group by one more person and extend the duration by five more minutes.

Your turn. Pick a goal that you would like to work on and come up with a plan of how you'll take action steps to achieve it. As you conquer any goal, place a check mark next to that item and give yourself some appreciation before going to the next goal.

Note: For bigger goals that require more time or effort, break them down to several smaller, intermediate goals.

_____

_____

_____

_____

CHAPTER 6

The Power of Forgiveness

How often do you find yourself thinking about the times you were hurt, mistreated, or rejected by others? When you replayed those events in your mind, how did it make you feel? What emotions came up for you?

Chances are when you thought of these events, you felt several strong emotions such as sadness, fear, disappointment, hurt, betrayal, inferiority, anger, powerlessness, loneliness, shame, or other equally negative feelings. Has it ever helped you to feel this way? For most people, the answer is "no."

In fact, you've probably experienced having your entire day ruined, not because of what happened that day, but because you spent so much time and energy feeling sorry for yourself or beating yourself up for what you should have or could have done differently. You wish you could let things go easily like others around you, but you can't seem to stop thinking about what happened and how people have hurt you. How can you forgive and move on when you can't stop reliving the pain in your head?

You are not alone in this pattern. As humans, it's easy for us to focus on and replay negative events. In fact, we are wired that way. Our life experiences have taught us to pay extra attention to negativities and hang onto the pain associated with them.

Ever since you were a little child, you have watched the people around you giving more attention to negative events and giving you the impression that negative events are worth paying special attention to.

Think about it for a moment.

There were countless times where you were happy playing by yourself and no one took notice. But the moment you hurt yourself, hurt someone else, or did something "bad" like throwing a tantrum, everyone around you rushed in to give you extra attention. Yes, some of that attention was negative, but it's still attention all the same.

Further, when something terrible happens, people talk about it more. If it's newsworthy, every channel on TV will be broadcasting the story repeatedly. You can't seem to get away from the story no matter how many times you've changed the channel.

Whether you know it or not, from events like these, your subconscious mind developed beliefs such as, "When I get hurt or do something bad, I get extra attention," or "Pain, trauma, and other unfortunate events are important. Pay attention to them." So, when something goes wrong or when someone hurts you, you hang onto those memories and replay them often.

Think of a time when you had a horrible experience at a restaurant. How many people did you share that experience with? What about a time when your restaurant experience was just so-so? How many people did you share that experience with? More likely than not, you told at least twice as many people about the negative experience as compared to the OK experience.

When you think about those two restaurant examples, how many details can you recall about each incidence? You are likely to recall many details from the terrible experience and not so many things about the so-so experience. This is because your mind is wired to pay attention to and remember negative events.

Remember your friend and assistant, the subconscious mind? It has a vital role in keeping painful memories fresh in your mind. Since its job is to keep you safe from danger (real or imagined), your subconscious mind will not only remember all of your painful experiences, but it will also continuously scan your surroundings for evidence of similar wrong-doings to prompt you to avoid certain people and situations.

Sadly, this causes you to be hyper-aware and sensitive to each instance where you perceive that people might be mistreating you, or when you are potentially doing something "wrong." This often leads you to misread situations and creates unnecessary pain for you.

Why Forgiveness is a Super Power

Stress, as you may know, is the number one cause of so many health problems such as high blood pressure, stomach problems, headaches, and depression. When you carry so much fear, doubt, or anger, whether at yourself or others, your stress level increases and it affects your overall health.

> Forgiveness is a key to lowering your stress and improving your quality of life.

Forgiveness liberates you from all that heavy burden (and subsequent stress!) while providing you with a clean slate to move forward.

Imagine this scenario for a moment. You just got into a terrible argument with a good friend and you feel like she was mean and hurtful to you. You tried to explain to her why you're feeling hurt and upset, but she just doesn't seem to get it. You become angrier as you withdraw inside yourself. Your friend is trying to make light of the situation and says, "Stop being so sensitive. Come to my party tonight. We'll have so much fun."

If you're hanging on to the hurt, chances are you would choose to stay home and not attend her party. You might even think, "I'm going to send her a clear message about how angry I am by not showing up to her stupid party."

So, instead of going to the party and having fun like you really wanted to, you stayed home and stewed in your anger and misery. Your friend, on the other hand, proceeded to have a great time at her party. She might think about you briefly and she might even feel sad for a moment that you're not there, but she most likely will be focused on the friends who are there and enjoying her time with them.

You wanted to make her pay, but in the end, who really suffered? You were so wrapped up in your pain and thoughts of making her pay that you couldn't enjoy yourself. You replayed the fight over and over, which caused you to be even more upset with your friend. You might even become so irritable that you yelled at your little brother when he asked you to play with him. You are now the one dishing out the pain and you didn't even realize it. How damaging is that?

Let's imagine that you decided to forgive your friend instead. It might feel a little awkward at first because you're not used to letting things go easily. However, because you have learned how to unleash some of your Inner Super Powers, you decided to go into your Personal Creation Studio and practice these new skills.

For thirty minutes straight, you practiced hanging out with your friend at her party, being fully present, and having fun. You practiced seeing yourself completely at ease, laughing with and connecting deeply with this friend and other friends at her party. As you practiced these new skills in your Studio, you also practiced a new ISP Command: "It's easy for me to forgive."

With these practices, you began to feel better about the situation and decided to attend her party. At the party, you noticed how much easier it was for you to have fun. Your friend was also very happy that you attended the party. She gave you a big hug and thanked you for being there.

You leave the party feeling good about yourself and your friendship and you bring that wonderful energy home with you. When your little brother asks you to play with him, you do so happily, and you two share a precious bonding moment.

Inspirational author Katherine Ponder[9] said something that I very much agree with: "When you hold resentment toward another, you are bound to that person or condition by an emotional link that is stronger than steel. Forgiveness is the only way to dissolve that link and get free."

When you choose to forgive, you stop wasting your time and energy rehashing the same old story and feeling sorry for yourself. That's the power of forgiveness.

> When you forgive, you set yourself free to enjoy the things that matter most to you.

You might be thinking, "OK, that makes sense, but what if I forgive someone and they don't change because they think I'm OK with what they did? Or worse yet, what if I forgive them and they think I'm

---

[9] http://www.azquotes.com/author/20507-Catherine_Ponder

weak and they take advantage of me even more? I don't want to be friends with someone like that."

While it's understandable that you might have these concerns, would you agree that all of these concerns are fear-based? If you want to destroy your fear and self-doubt, you can choose to shift your energy away from the familiar fear-based thoughts and focus on your Inner Super Powers instead.

When you forgive, it doesn't mean that you have agreed with what happened, nor does it mean that you've excused their actions. All it means is that you've accepted that the situation occurred and there's nothing you can do to change the past, so you're choosing to focus on the present moment and the future.

Maybe it's a simple misunderstanding and you can quickly clear things up by having a meaningful conversation that deepens your relationship. Maybe there's a great lesson or two that you can learn from that experience that will help you to grow as a person. When you forgive, the act of forgiveness is really for you and not so much for the other person.

Yes, it would be nice if they can understand what they did and change their future behavior because of it. However, the decision to change is entirely up to them. You have no control over that, regardless of how much time, energy, and effort you spend trying to make it happen. The more you try to control or manipulate the situation, the longer you stay trapped and bound to this person. It's almost as if you gave them the power to control how you feel.

Instead, you can decide to forgive that person and move forward. In doing so, you reclaim your power. It's like you're declaring, "Enough! You can't control me anymore. I'm in charge of how I feel and how I spend my time."

Forgiveness also doesn't mean that you have to be friends with that person. Just as the other person has the choice whether to change, you have a choice in whether you want to maintain that relationship. Forgiveness just means letting go of the negativity so you can move forward, with or without that person in your life.

So far, we've been talking about forgiving others and how that frees you. Let's talk about another side of forgiveness that is equally important, but often overlooked, and that's self-forgiveness.

For a moment, think of something you did that you still feel regret, guilt, or shame about. Or maybe think of a time when you let yourself or someone else down, or somehow simply disappointed yourself. How do these events and the feelings attached to them hold you back? Does it feel heavy and burdensome to carry all of those self-judgments around with you? Wouldn't it be nice to start fresh and move forward without that burden?

If you want a fresh start, you can begin by forgiving yourself. Just like forgiving others, forgiving yourself does not mean that you are OK with what you did. Self-forgiveness means you've recognized that what you did was not desirable and you're willing to let it go so you can spend your energy on discovering ways to improve that situation or make up with someone that you may have hurt.

How to Destroy Fear and Self-Doubt Using the Power of Forgiveness

How does forgiveness help you to destroy your fear and self-doubt? Holding onto feelings of hurt, anger, or resentment only makes you feel worse about yourself and your situation and ultimately causes you to second-guess and doubt yourself. You might feel like a victim. You might feel all alone in this world. It's no wonder that you would want to protect yourself from future pain.

But what happens when you try to defend yourself? Usually, self-protection means thinking about and remembering the act that caused you pain, in hopes of avoiding a repeat of it in the future. It also means having to close yourself up to some degree.

Maybe you've been rejected or betrayed by a friend, so now, you're afraid to open up and let people get to know the real you. Perhaps you've been teased by others for expressing yourself, so now, you hold back from saying what you want to say. Perhaps you've failed at something important to you and now, you no longer attempt to take on meaningful challenges out of fear of repeating the failure.

Let's say you've been picked on by a classmate and now, you're afraid to be around that person. What kind of thoughts do you have when that person is near you? Do you show up as a happy, confident, and carefree person? Or do you show up as angry, timid, and a bit awkward? Are you showing up in a way that makes it difficult for someone to tease you, or are you showing up as an "easy target?"

I'm not suggesting that it's your fault that you were teased. You are definitely NOT at fault. Bullies will be bullies and you cannot control that. What you do have control over is how you feel and how you present yourself to others.

Remember, your subconscious mind is always working to give you more of your current experience. When you focus on how this person has teased you and caused you pain, your subconscious mind will be looking for evidence of the same. This causes you to be on high alert and fearful.

Remember the chapter about the Inner Super Power of Your Body? In that chapter, you learned that when your mind is running a "weak program" such as fear, your body will naturally close up, making you look small and not very confident. All of these factors work together against you, making it easier for bullies to continue to pick on you. The good news is that you can change this pattern.

Imagine you've decided to forgive the person that picked on you and let go of the negativities. Rather than taking what they said or did personally, you recognize that this person is dealing with their own stuff and was just taking it out on you. That doesn't make the situation right, but it puts the situation in a different perspective for you, doesn't it? How would you show up differently now? What thoughts would you have?

The next time you see that person, rather than feeling fearful, you might feel neutral or better yet, even compassionate toward them. Because you are no longer focusing on fear, your mind and your body will respond appropriately and you will appear completely different to others.

When you focus your energy on protecting yourself, you limit your positive energy and limit your ability to be in the present moment.

> Remember, fear exists only in your imagination. Fear is created by recalling events from the past or imagining events in the future. Fear does not exist in the present moment.

When you get out of your head and focus on what is in front of you, you eliminate your fear and self-doubt. When you don't have to worry so much about how to act, what to say, or how to protect yourself, you will feel better and stronger overall. Your self-esteem and confidence automatically increase. You can relax, be yourself, and enjoy the people around you and the environment that you're in.

In addition, forgiveness can help you develop and strengthen your other Inner Super Powers, as well as restore your peace of mind. How powerful is that?

NOTE: Forgiveness work can be challenging for many. While the following exercises are helpful to release unwanted emotions, they are not meant to replace professional help. If your situation is difficult to handle, or you don't know how to proceed on your own, please talk to your parents or a trusted adult and ask for help.

You can also do a search for "teen crisis" with your city and state for local resources. For example, "teen crisis Asheville North Carolina."

Self-Reflection

Forgiving Others

1. Think of a person or situation that you still hold anger or resentment for. Write down key relevant information. (**NOTE**: Since you will be addressing very personal issues with the exercises in this chapter, you might want to write your answers in a separate notebook or journal.)

_____

_____

_____

_____

_____

_____

_____

_____

_____

_____

_____

_____

_____

_____

_____

_____

_____

2. How is holding on to the negativity and pain from this event holding you back? What has it prevented you from doing? What might it have caused you to do that you otherwise wouldn't have?

_____

_____

_____

_____

_____

_____

_____

_____

_____

_____

_____

_____

3. Are you afraid that something bad would happen if you were to forgive this person or situation? Go ahead and express any fear you might have.

_____

_____

_____

_____

_____

_____

_____

_____

_____

_____

_____

4. How can forgiving this person or situation improve your life? What are you now free to do, think, or feel without the weight of this issue?

_____

_____

_____

_____

_____

_____

_____

_____

_____

_____

_____

_____

_____

_____

_____

_____

_____

_____

_____

_____

_____

_____

5. Take a moment to notice how liberating it feels to let go of the weight of this problem. With your forgiveness, you have the power to give yourself this magnificent gift of freedom to move forward.

Forgiving Yourself

1. Think of something that you've done that you feel regret, guilt, or shame about. Write down all the relevant details.

_____

_____

_____

_____

_____

_____

_____

_____

_____

_____

_____

_____

_____

_____

_____

_____

_____

_____

_____

_____

_____

_____

_____

_____

_____

2. As you were thinking about and writing down details of that event, how did it make you feel? What thoughts did you have?

_____

_____

_____

_____

_____

_____

_____

_____

_____

_____

_____

_____

_____

3. Why haven't you forgiven yourself?

_____

_____

_____

_____

_____

_____

_____

_____

_____

_____

_____

_____

_____

_____

4. What are you afraid would happen if you forgave yourself?

_____

_____

_____

_____

_____

_____

_____

_____

_____

_____

_____

_____

_____

_____

5. What can you learn from this event?

_____

_____

_____

_____

_____

_____

_____

_____

_____

_____

_____

_____

_____

6. How can you use what you've learned to help yourself be a better person?

_____

_____

_____

_____

_____

_____

_____

_____

_____

_____

_____

_____

_____

_____

_____

_____

_____

_____

_____

_____

_____

Spend a few minutes envisioning this improved version of yourself, having learned a powerful lesson. Give yourself permission to embrace this lesson and move forward now.

Tapping into the ISP of Forgiveness

Exercise One: Write a Letter

We often try to ignore or suppress our undesirable feelings to avoid dealing with them. This causes the unwanted feelings to grow and fester until we explode unexpectedly.

This letter-writing exercise will help you to reconnect with those buried feelings so you can let them go in a healthy way. For this exercise to work best, be completely honest in expressing your feelings. No one will read this letter but you. Write down everything you're thinking, feeling, and wanting to say.

Here is your chance to express yourself and your feelings without any negative consequences. You can use this method to forgive yourself or forgive others.

Step One:
Think of someone who has hurt you. Pick someone who may be easiest for you to forgive. Just like any other skill, forgiveness is something you can get better at with practice. To give you the best chance of mastering this essential skill, start with the smaller issues, and build up to those you perceive as major issues as you develop this Inner Super Power.

If you prefer to start by working on forgiving yourself first, start with a small wrongdoing and work up to the bigger ones. You'll find it becomes easier and easier to let go of your judgments with a bit of practice.

Step Two:

Grab a piece of paper and a pen and start writing that person (or yourself) a letter. (Don't worry; you won't have to send this letter to them for this to work.) Start with, *"Dear _____,"* and let your feelings flow freely onto the page. Focus on your thoughts and feelings. Using proper grammar is not important for this exercise. You don't even have to write in full sentences if you don't want to. Write down all the feelings you've been carrying around with you, as well the feelings you have at this moment. If you've been holding onto sadness, fear, anger or hatred, write them down.

Give yourself permission to say everything that's on your mind and in your heart. This is your opportunity to get everything off your chest and to free yourself of the burden of having to carry these emotions with you any farther into your future.

Some people report experiencing strong emotions as they are doing this exercise. This is very normal, as you are bringing up emotions you might have been trying to hide or ignore for a long time. Allow these feelings to come up. If you feel like crying, cry. It's good to let it out.

Step Three:

Once you are done writing down all the things you think and feel, then move onto forgiveness. Write down why you are choosing to forgive and how you are ready to move forward.

If you're having a hard time writing about forgiveness, you can start by using the following paragraph and fill in your own details.

_____, *I choose to forgive you. I'm not saying what you did was OK. I just don't need to hold onto this burden anymore. I can't be* _____ *(insert your negative emotion here) and be free and happy at the same time. I choose to be free and happy. I deserve to be free and happy. I forgive you now.*

In the case of self-forgiveness, you might consider:

I forgive myself. I have allowed my guilt, anger, and fear to control me for far too long. I am realizing I do not need to feel bad about the past to make good decisions moving forward. I am committed to learning from my past and to always work on becoming a better version of myself. I forgive myself completely for my mistake. I love who I have become today. I am ready to move forward peacefully. I deserve to be free and happy.

Step Four:

Many people find it liberating to tear this letter up after they are done writing it. They feel that they have already expressed themselves when they wrote the letter and don't feel a need to revisit the story. If this is what you choose to do, as you tear up the letter, it's good to focus on forgiveness and letting things go. You might even say (out loud or in your head), "I'm choosing to forgive. It feels good to forgive. I deserve to be free. I am free."

If you prefer not to tear the letter up, go ahead and put it away for now so you can focus on forgiveness. Imagine going into your Studio and forgiving yourself or the person who has caused you pain.

You might choose to review the letter at a different time to see how your feeling has changed and see what new insights you have developed. However, if you still feel strong negative emotions when you reread the letter, know that there's more work to be done. Choose one of the other exercises mentioned to continue your work on letting go of this situation completely.

Exercise Two: Avoid the Blame Game

Another very useful way to forgive yourself or others is to remove the blame. Rather than focusing on who's to blame, shift your focus on evaluating the situation in a non-judgmental way with the goal of improving the outcome. Blaming yourself or others will only make the problem seem bigger. Focus on a win-win solution and take purposeful actions to resolve your problem instead.

You can use these four simple questions to guide yourself toward a solution.

1. What went wrong in this situation?
2. What went right in this situation?
3. What can I learn from this situation?
4. How can I improve the outcome of this situation?

Remember, it's very easy to miss the positive aspects and the learning opportunities in events that you view as "bad." Challenge yourself to view each situation as an opportunity to grow and focus on building-up your strengths. Even a situation as difficult as being bullied can have tremendous learning opportunities. Perhaps you can choose to become more empathetic and compassionate toward others because of your experiences.

If you seem stuck on what went wrong, you can use this additional question to guide you away from the negativities.

1. How would _____ (insert the name of someone you admire) view this situation?

Let's practice removing blame by working through a situation using these same questions.

1. Think of a situation that you still hold negative feelings toward. This could be a conflict with a friend or with yourself. Write down the relevant details here.

_____

_____

_____

_____

_____

_____

_____

_____

_____

_____

_____

_____

_____

_____

_____

_____

_____

_____

_____

_____

_____

_____

2. What went wrong in this situation?

_____

_____

_____

_____

_____

_____

_____

_____

_____

_____

_____

_____

_____

3. What went right in this situation?

_____

_____

_____

_____

_____

_____

_____

_____

_____

_____

_____

_____

_____

4. What can I learn from this situation?

_____

_____

_____

_____

_____

_____

_____

_____

_____

_____

_____

_____

_____

5. How can I improve the outcome of this situation?

_____

_____

_____

_____

_____

_____

_____

_____

_____

_____

_____

_____

6. How has my point of view changed as a result of this exercise?

_____

_____

_____

_____

_____

_____

_____

_____

_____

_____

_____

_____

_____

If using those four questions did not change your point of view, go on to the next question.

7. How would _____ (insert the name of someone you admire) view this situation?

_____

_____

_____

_____

_____

_____

_____

_____

_____

_____

8. How have your feelings changed now that you've looked at the same situation in a different way, or through the eyes of someone you admire?

_____

_____

_____

_____

_____

_____

_____

_____

_____

_____

_____

_____

_____

_____

_____

_____

_____

_____

_____

_____

_____

_____

_____

_____

_____

_____

_____

_____

Exercise Three: Personal Creation Studio

Forgiving Others:

Imagine going into your Studio and practice forgiving that person. Practice saying what you want to say and doing what you want to do. Vividly see yourself so relaxed and completely comfortable with letting things go. If you have chosen to rebuild the relationship, see your relationship the way you would like it to be. If you want to let go of the relationship, see yourself free from this relationship and being completely at ease with that decision. Remember, you are safe in your Studio. You can "try out" different ways of forgiving until you find a way that feels good to you.

Forgiving Yourself:

Imagine going into your Studio and practice forgiving yourself. Vividly see yourself so relaxed and completely comfortable with letting things go. Focus on the lesson you have learned from this experience. How can you use this information to help you become a better person? Visualize whatever you would like to have happen next. Give yourself permission to do what you've been wanting to do. If you need to make it up to someone, what would you like to do? Practice seeing yourself taking steps to rebuild your relationship with anyone you may have hurt, or the relationship with yourself.

Write down any thoughts or feelings that might come up for you as you work in your Studio.

_____

_____

_____

_____

_____

_____

_____

_____

_____

_____

_____

_____

_____

_____

_____

_____

_____

_____

_____

_____

_____

_____

_____

_____

_____

_____

_____

_____

_____

CHAPTER 7

The Power of Love

L ove is a primary and essential human need. There are thousands of songs about love. There are thousands of movies about love. Human lives are conceived as a result of love. Love conquers all. Love makes the world go 'round.

Indeed, there is no shortage of inspiration for words to describe love and the effects of love. Without love and nurturing, we can't thrive. We crave the feeling of being loved and we enjoy showing love to those we care about. Love fills us with a sense of comfort, belonging, and safety. When we have love, life is easier and more meaningful. When we lack love, life seems lonely and cold.

Let's do a quick check-in on the love you have in your life. Stop reading this book and for the next five minutes, grab a piece of paper and make a list of all the people you love. Do take the time to create this list before continuing with the rest of this chapter. This is an important step to assessing your Power of Love. Go ahead; grab a piece of paper and a pen or pencil. Set your timer for five minutes and go! Just create your list freely and write down whoever comes to mind.

Now, take a look at the list. At what point did you mention yourself? Are you toward the top of your list, somewhere in the middle, or at the very bottom? Did you even make it on your own list?

It is common for people to forget to include themselves on their "People I love" list because they focus their love outwardly. When they think of giving and receiving love, they think it's an act coming from themselves to someone else, or from someone else to them.

Others feel uncomfortable with the idea of self-love, fearing they might appear arrogant or self-centered. Still, others feel unlovable or see themselves as being undeserving of self-love.

Where are you on this spectrum? Do you show yourself the same level of kindness, love, and respect that you show others, or do you treat yourself poorly in these areas? Do you make time for yourself as you do for others?

While it's a wonderful trait to love others and to treat others with love, it is equally, if not more important to love yourself.

To fully experience the Power of Love, you need to start from within and develop a strong feeling of love for yourself. In this chapter, when we talk about love, we're talking about self-love. When you love yourself deeply, giving love to and receiving love from others will be a breeze.

Why Love is a Super Power

When you think of self-love, what is the first thing that comes to mind? Do you get excited at the thought of being able to show yourself how important and deserving you are? Or does the idea of taking the time to care for yourself and your needs feel foreign and uncomfortable for you?

If it puts a smile on your face when you think about showing yourself love, then you're ahead of the curve. Go ahead and continue to show yourself just how magnificent you are!

If it makes you uncomfortable to think of self-love, let's work together to change that. You deserve to love yourself and to treat yourself with respect, kindness, and compassion.

Why would something as simple and beneficial as practicing self-love be so uncommon and difficult for many? Part of that answer may lie within our culture's definition of self-love[10]: "1. Conceit 2. Regard for one's own happiness or advantage."

Given that part of the definition of self-love is "conceit" and "regard for one's own advantage," it's no wonder so many people are uncomfortable with the concept of loving themselves. After all, who wants to be seen as a conceited person or one who only regards things for their advantage? Consequently, instead of showing ourselves love and creating our own

---

[10] "self-love." Merriam-Webster.com. 2017. https://www.merriam-webster.com (7 November 2017).

happiness, we give love to others and we depend on others to give us love and to make us happy.

What if, instead of focusing on those aspects of the definition of self-love, we decided to accept that self-love is "regard for one's own happiness?"

For the next few minutes, imagine that you have the total freedom to focus on creating your personal happiness. To be clear, when I say, "freedom to focus on creating your personal happiness," I do mean freedom to do what you want for yourself, as long as you're not purposefully breaking the law or hurting someone else.

What would that look like for you? How would you think, act, or feel differently when your decisions are based solely on your happiness and not pleasing someone else—nor being concerned about what others may think of how you spend your time? How liberating does it feel to leave behind the fear, self-doubt, negative judgment, regret, shame, and guilt?

That's exactly what self-love can do for you. It can fill you with wonderful feelings that motivate you to live your life to the fullest. At a deep level, we all want to feel loved and to know that we are deserving of love. We all want to be able to show ourselves love; so, why is it so hard for most people to show self-love?

The following three misguided beliefs are often cited as the reasons why many people are uncomfortable making self-love a priority.

Misguided Beliefs
1. It's Selfish to Focus on Your Needs

Chances are, early on in your life, the act of self-love and doing what makes you happy was very natural to you. Imagine these scenarios.

You were blissfully minding your own business and doing what feels good to you, instead of allowing your sibling to pressure you to do what you don't want to do. Your sibling got mad at you and angrily accused you of being thoughtless, inconsiderate, or selfish.

Maybe another time you were scolded because you told your parents you wanted to go to your friend's house as planned, instead of staying home to babysit your siblings. Perhaps your parents yelled at you and told you how disappointed they were with you. They said that a good person would think about others' feelings and would sacrifice their needs to make them happy.

Maybe you were told that you should be ashamed of always wanting things your way. Guilt, shame, and a load of other heavy burdens were placed upon you and you learned just how much that hurts.

Your subconscious mind was paying close attention, as it always does. It recorded this whole painful exchange and it will use it to help protect you from similar painful experiences in the future. The next time you think about doing what makes you happy, your subconscious mind kicks in to protect you and replays this and other similar movies.

You'll start feeling uneasy as you second-guess yourself with questions such as, "Is what I want really all that important? Am I being thoughtless, inconsiderate, or selfish?"

And as you think about those thoughts and feel the anxiety around them, you decide to go ahead and do what the other person wanted. And for that, you get rewarded. Your parents told you how proud they are that you're thinking about other people's feelings. They tell you that you're such a good person and rewarded you with extra attention, love, or other tokens of appreciation.

After a few of these incidences, you began to grow up believing:

- Doing what I want is thoughtless, inconsiderate, and selfish.
- It's more important to make other people happy than to make myself happy.
- When I sacrifice my needs, I am appreciated by others.

2. You're Not Worthy of Good Things in Life

These beliefs were intensified by other experiences in your life that caused you to feel as though you weren't deserving of good things. Perhaps in the heat of anger, your parents yelled at you to stop wasting time on "useless" things (things that you loved doing) because you should focus on bringing your grades up and helping with chores around the house.

Or maybe you've heard your parents talk about all the sacrifices they have made to provide for you and your siblings, and that made you feel guilty. Maybe a friend or two ended their friendships with you because you didn't do what they wanted to do.

Then, of course, there were all the times that you beat yourself up for messing up or letting yourself or others down. Experiences like these reinforced your belief that your desires and needs are not that important and that you are not worthy of them. To conform to what is expected of you and earn the title of being "worthy," you focus your attention on meeting others' needs while neglecting your own.

When you continue to ignore your own needs, you lose connection to who you are and to what makes you feel good. This causes your self-esteem to plummet and your dissatisfaction with yourself (and your life) to worsen.

3. You Are Unlovable Because You Are Flawed

Even when you have the time to focus on your needs, you may have a hard time showing yourself love because you can't stop focusing on your perceived flaws. This causes you to feel unworthy and undeserving of love and happiness.

Here's a common scenario among teens. See if you can relate to this, or a similar situation. There is a special occasion coming up; maybe a school dance or a friend's party, and you're so excited to attend. You found the perfect outfit and your hair looks great. But this morning you woke up with a large pimple on your face.

Instead of admiring yourself for how great you look and focusing on the fun event, you focus all of your attention on the pimple. Instead of being present and enjoying yourself, you're stuck in your head, thinking about your pimple, which causes you to feel insecure about how you look. At the gathering, you find it hard to enjoy yourself because you're certain that everyone is staring at your pimple and judging you.

If you often feel this way, I have some news for you. You're a human being. As long as you're a human being, you'll have perceived flaws. There's just no way around it. If you wait until you think you are perfect before loving yourself, you'll lose out on an incredible opportunity for happiness and fulfillment right now.

Loving yourself does not mean that you believe you are perfect or that you always do things perfectly. Loving yourself means that you choose to accept yourself exactly as you are, flaws and all.

> Showing yourself love and being kind to yourself are two of the best things you can do to build your self-confidence and self-esteem and change your life for the better.

When you love yourself, you release the constant pressure of having to make others happy and the heavy burden of living with endless self-doubt and self-judgments.

Without the pressure, doubts, and judgment, you'll have the freedom and peace of mind to explore things you enjoy, which helps you to grow as a person. When you know who you are and you feel good about yourself, it is much easier to make positive decisions for yourself.

Self-love also acts as a natural anti-depressant and a natural anti-anxiety. The more you love yourself and treat yourself with kindness, the easier it will be to tap into your strength and stay calm and clear-minded during difficult situations.

Self-love also makes bouncing back from these types of events easier. When you practice self-love consistently, you'll become a happier, healthier person with a strong sense of self-worth. Your ability to give and receive love deepens because you now see yourself as a good person who is deserving of love.

How to Destroy Fear and Self-Doubt Using the Power of Love

For a moment, think about how you've been treating yourself when your fear and self-doubt are high. Have you been showing yourself love, or have you been showing disrespect or disregard for yourself? In those moments, are the words you're using to yourself supportive and kind, or do you find yourself making the situation worse by calling yourself names and berating yourself for your perceived flaws?

Think about the words you say to yourself in these situations. Would you ever say these same words to a friend, a family member, or even a stranger when they are already down on themselves? Would it be OK to talk to others this way?

Chances are, if you're honest with yourself, the answer is an easy NO! It is not OK to speak to others the way you speak to yourself when you're upset. If you talk to others the way you talk to yourself, you wouldn't have too many friends. People would think you're mean, abusive, or a bully.

And yet, somehow, you feel it's okay to talk to yourself in this manner. These kinds of self-talk show a big disregard for yourself and reinforce your belief that you are unworthy or undeserving of love. This is not exactly a great foundation for showing yourself love.

Instead of beating yourself up the next time you feel fear or self-doubt, what if you tapped into your Inner Super Power of Words to give yourself love and support? One way you can show yourself love is to challenge yourself to treat yourself with the same level of thoughtfulness, kindness, and respect that you show the person you love most.

If you can't imagine saying any words to this person, avoid saying them to yourself. If it makes you feel good to use these words with that person, start using those words to yourself. You can choose positive Word Filters such as:

"Slow down. Breathe. You've got it."

"I believe in you."

"Everything will be OK."

"Let's figure out how to solve this problem."

"You can do it!"

You can also go into your Personal Creation Studio and practice solving whatever problem you're facing with courage, confidence, and self-belief. Use your imagination to vividly see yourself conquering your problems in several creative ways.

When you practice trusting yourself and your abilities, your confidence skyrockets. You'll find it easier to courageously face your problems and follow your dreams. How you feel about yourself and the words you use when you talk to yourself become highly positive.

With practice, you'll find it easier to prioritize yourself and your needs. Your subconscious mind will help you achieve your dreams by helping you to focus on the important aspects of yourself. You can practice self-love by forgiving yourself and accepting your short-comings while giving yourself permission to see the best in yourself.

When you show yourself that kind of love, support, and encouragement, how does it feel? What would you be able to do differently?

In addition to showing yourself love in moments of fear and self-doubt, what if you decided to show yourself love daily by choosing activities that relax you, inspire you, and recharge you? When you make the conscious decision to nurture your body, heart, and spirit, you leave very little room left for fear and self-doubt. After all, if you feel good about yourself and you see your flaws or failures as opportunities for growth, what is there to be afraid of?

When you treat yourself as a person who deserves love, kindness, and respect, you are showing others how to treat you.

Engaging in self-care daily helps you to release your stress, gives you more energy, and helps you to look and feel your best so you can be happy with yourself and your life.

Remember to include some self-love activities that might not feel very fun, but that you know are important for your overall health and happiness, such as eating healthy.

Self-Reflection

1. In the beginning of the chapter, you created a list of people that you love. Did you make it onto your own list? How did you feel when you discovered that showing yourself love is just as important as showing love for anyone else?

_____

_____

_____

_____

_____

_____

_____

_____

2. Think of a time when you felt upset or disappointed with yourself and you used harsh, damaging words as you talked to yourself. What words did you use? What names did you call yourself?

_____

_____

_____

_____

_____

_____

_____

_____

3. How did those words and names make you feel?

_____

_____

_____

_____

_____

_____

_____

_____

_____

_____

_____

_____

_____

4. What was the outcome of that situation? Was it resolved, or does it still linger for you?

_____

_____

_____

_____

_____

_____

_____

_____

_____

_____

_____

_____

_____

5. Now, think about that same situation again; this time, with love and kindness for yourself. Imagine your thoughts and self-talk through these Word Filters. What words did you choose to speak to yourself this time?

_____

_____

_____

_____

_____

_____

_____

_____

_____

_____

_____

6. How do these words make you feel differently?

_____

_____

_____

_____

_____

_____

_____

_____

_____

_____

_____

_____

7. How do you think the outcome would have been improved if you had spoken to yourself with these words when you first encountered this issue?

_____

_____

_____

_____

_____

_____

_____

_____

_____

_____

_____

_____

_____

8. List two to three things you currently do consistently to show yourself love. They don't need to be grand gestures, or even highly time-consuming. Using positive and caring self-talk and allowing yourself to simply learn when mistakes are made are great examples.

_____

_____

_____

_____

_____

_____

9. Create a list of ten things you could do to show yourself love in the future. Remember, even little things you do that are good for you or allow you the space to feel special are great. Anything counts here, no matter how small or how large, as long as you are showing yourself love in the process.

Example: eat an apple instead of a bag of chips, take a twenty-minute walk after dinner, listen to music, play with your dog, buy yourself something nice, practice ISP Commands, meditate, etc.

_____

_____

_____

_____

_____

_____

_____

_____

_____

_____

_____

_____

_____

_____

_____

_____

_____

_____

_____

_____

_____

10. Now that you are aware of the Inner Super Power of Love, are you willing to start showing yourself love on a daily basis? Make that commitment to yourself now. You can place a sticky note by your phone or nightstand as a daily reminder to engage in this vital self-care activity. You can even wear a special ring or another piece of accessory you like, as a symbol of your commitment to show yourself love each day.

Tapping into the ISP of Love

Exercise One: I LOVE ME!

<u>Step One:</u>

Set a timer for five minutes and write down everything you dislike about yourself and things you wish that you could change about yourself if you could.

_____

_____

_____

_____

_____

_____

_____

_____

_____

_____

_____

_____

_____

_____

_____

_____

_____

_____

_____

_____

_____

_____

Step Two:

Set a timer for another five minutes and write down everything you love or admire about yourself. Again, everything counts… nothing is too small to list here.

_____

_____

_____

_____

_____

_____

_____

_____

_____

_____

_____

_____

_____

_____

_____

_____

_____

_____

_____

_____

_____

_____

_____

_____

_____

_____

Step Three:

Add up your lists and write the numbers below.
- I have _____ items on my "things I dislike or wish I could change about myself" list.
- I have _____ items on my "things I love or admire about myself" list.

Do your numbers surprise you? For many people, it is very difficult to come up with just ten things they love or admire about themselves. Yet, it is so easy to come up with more than ten things they don't like about themselves. How do you think this affects the relationship you have with yourself?

Did you know that the quality of every single relationship you will ever have depends on the relationship you have with yourself? What that means is if you don't love who you are and don't believe that you are lovable, how can you expect anyone else to love you? If you don't have love for yourself first, how can you continue to give love to another person? You know what they say about how you can't give what you don't have?

Imagine your self-love is like a battery that needs charging—just like your smartphone battery. If you have a full charge, you can easily give love to others and have high-quality relationships as a result. But if your self-love battery is low or empty, there isn't any love to share in your relationships. So, if you want to give and receive love at a true and deep level, you must start with loving yourself first.

In addition, your subconscious mind is constantly looking for evidence that matches your belief system. If you believe that you are unlovable or undeserving of love, your subconscious mind will work hard to give you that experience. Therefore, even though you might have great love for someone, your mind will point out to you all the instances that look like this person doesn't love you back. This might cause you to work unrealistically hard to make this person happy, so you can "earn" their love.

You give, then give some more, until there's little left to give (your love battery is beyond drained). Still, your subconscious mind focuses on finding evidence that you don't have the love you want. This causes you to feel a range of emotions from sadness, to feeling as though you're being used or disrespected, to anger and disappointment. You can easily be overtaken by these strong emotions, causing you to doubt that person and to doubt yourself.

Because you didn't believe that you were lovable, you couldn't feel love from others, which led to feelings that could harm your relationship. You can change this damaging pattern by charging up your own love battery first—and continuously each day.

Step Four:

Let's start working on creating that fantastic relationship with yourself and making sure you know how to effectively charge your self-love battery.

Set a timer for twenty minutes this time. Write down everything you love about yourself and your life.

Nothing is too small or too minor of an item for this list. Write down the things you've done that you are proud of, the things you're good at, and any accomplishments you've achieved. Write down your personality traits and physical attributes that you love. Write down compliments others have given you.

Remember to add quirky things you love about yourself and your life as well.

Here is a list to inspire you:

1. I love my sense of humor.
2. I love how long my hair is.
3. I love that I have freckles on the tip of my nose.
4. I love that I love animals.
5. I love that I can dance.
6. I love that I have small feet.
7. I love my smile.
8. I love being the youngest in my family.
9. I love that I make the best ice cream sundae.
10. I love that I have friends from different parts of the world because of social media.
11. I love that I have a fast metabolism.
12. I love that I have all my teeth.
13. I love my commitment to living green.
14. I love that I'm in honors classes.
15. I love that I'm a good friend.
16. I love that I stopped biting my nails.
17. I love that I'm really good at solving mysteries.
18. I love that my ears look like elf ears.
19. I love that I can play the drum.
20. I love that people think I'm a thoughtful person.

Go ahead and create your own I Love Me! list.

_____

_____

_____

_____

_____

_____

_____

_____

_____

_____

_____

_____

_____

_____

_____

_____

_____

_____

_____

_____

_____

_____

_____

_____

_____

_____

_____

_____

_____

_____

_____

_____

_____

_____

_____

_____

_____

_____

_____

_____

_____

_____

_____

_____

_____

_____

_____

_____

_____

_____

_____

_____

_____

_____

_____

_____

Step Five:

For the next two weeks, add at least three more items to your "I Love Me" list daily. Feel free to extend this exercise beyond two weeks if you wish.

Step Six:

Spend ten minutes each day enjoying your list. If you ever feel down about yourself or need a quick pick-me-up, go back to your list and review it again to remind yourself just how magnificent you really are. Pick one or two things you love about yourself and focus on those qualities.

Exercise Two:
Self-Care Activities to Feed Your Soul

When we have a lot on our plate and there's too much to do, the first thing that tends to go away is our self-care time—if we had any on our list to begin with! Self-care activities are actions you take that help you to feel recharged, energized, happy, relaxed, or taken care of.

Imagine you have a midterm to study for and you feel really behind. You're just certain that unless you study all day and all night this weekend, you'll fail the test. You have spent the past few hours in front of your book, trying your hardest to study, but nothing is making sense. You can't remember what you read, so you reread the same paragraph four times. You want to take a quick nap, but you just don't have time for it.

During moments like this, have you taken time to do the things you love—things that center you and help you to relax and feel good about yourself? If you are like most people, there's a really good chance that you haven't done that under such circumstances.

Now, imagine this scenario instead. You are behind and you need to study throughout the whole weekend to pass your midterms. You make a schedule to study and within that schedule, you include some breaks to relax and recharge.

For every two hours you spend studying, you take a fifteen-minute break. During that break, you do things you really enjoy. Maybe you take a brisk walk, chill out and watch YouTube videos, text your friends, or take a power nap. You'll even set a timer for fifteen minutes, so you don't get too side-tracked.

When you return to your studying, how do you think you'll do? Would you still have a hard time focusing, or would that fifteen minutes away from your studies recharge you with renewed energy?

Step One:

Spend the next ten to fifteen minutes and make a list of self-care activities that feed your soul and help you to feel happy, relaxed, energized, or motivated. Just like the "I Love Me!" list, add to this list often.

_____

_____

_____

_____

_____

_____

_____

_____

_____

_____

_____

_____

_____

_____

_____

_____

_____

_____

_____

_____

_____

_____

_____

_____

_____

_____

_____

_____

_____

_____

_____

_____

_____

_____

_____

_____

_____

_____

_____

_____

_____

_____

_____

_____

<u>Step Two:</u>

Make a commitment to spend at least twenty minutes each day on one or more of the self-care items you have on your list. Remember, when things are hectic, these activities become even more important to ease your mind and recharge your energy, so you can efficiently tackle the work ahead.

These are not selfish or "nice to have" activities. They are essential aspects of self-care and self-love. Being committed to good self-care will help you to be happier and more effective in everything you do.

Record how you feel when you engage in activities from your self-care list.

_____

_____

_____

_____

_____

_____

_____

_____

_____

_____

_____

_____

_____

_____

_____

_____

_____

_____

Exercise Three: ISP Command Revisited

<u>Step One:</u>

Spend the next few minutes writing down the things you would love to hear from others. It could be a compliment, an acknowledgement, an apology, or an encouragement.

_____

_____

_____

_____

_____

_____

_____

_____

_____

_____

_____

_____

_____

_____

_____

_____

_____

_____

_____

_____

_____

_____

_____

_____

Step Two:

Just because you haven't heard it from someone else doesn't mean you can't give those words to yourself. Look at your list above and pick out one or two phrases to give yourself daily while looking directly at yourself in the mirror. You can do this with an "I am statement" or a "You are" statement.

For example, let's say you would love for someone to compliment you with, "You are so smart." Look at yourself in the mirror and imagine you are looking at someone you really love and admire. Next, with meaning and purpose, tell yourself "You are so smart!" Maybe you want to wink at or smile at yourself. Maybe you want to give yourself a high-five or a double thumbs-up. Act the same way you would act if you were giving this compliment to someone else.

If you prefer, you can change that to an ISP Command of, "I'm so smart!" Both statements work great to reprogram your mind.

As a bonus, you can supercharge your Inner Super Powers by giving compliments to someone else. Chances are they would love hearing your kind and thoughtful words—and it just feels good to brighten someone's day. Giving others a compliment doesn't cost you anything, but it could make a significant difference in that person's day and boost their self-esteem. It could even enhance your relationship with them!

It's amazing to see what comes back to you when your self-love battery is full and you can genuinely give to others. This is one of the fastest ways to quick-charge your self-love battery!

CHAPTER 8

The Power of Perseverance

We all have plans that don't turn out as we intend, dreams that fall apart, and changes that are beyond our control. Setbacks, changes, and obstacles are all a part of life—a part that no one can completely avoid.

How do some people face these tough and ever-changing situations and still come out ahead, while others crumble at the slightest thought of such challenges? What is their secret? How do they keep moving forward when others just want to quit when the pressure becomes higher?

The secret ingredient for the people who keep pushing on when things get tough is perseverance. Some people were born with the ability to persevere and they can power through even the most challenging situations with seeming ease.

Perseverance is defined as "a steady persistence in a course of action, a purpose, a state, etc., especially in spite of difficulties, obstacles, or discouragement.[11]" How we

---

[11] "perseverance." Merriam-Webster.com. 2017. https://www.merriam-webster.com (7 November 2017).

deal with the constant unpredictable events in our life depends largely on our attitude, our belief systems, and our commitment to ourselves.

Maybe perseverance is not something that comes naturally to you, and the idea of pushing through difficulty sounds downright scary or even impossible to you right now. Luckily for you, perseverance, like all other ISPs, can be learned and strengthened with practice.

Having perseverance can mean the difference between turning your problems into opportunities or allowing your fear and judgments to cause you anxiety and keep you stuck. Given that the average person has challenges and unexpected curve-balls thrown at them every day, knowing how to deal with these situations positively will help you to move forward rather than becoming held back.

How you view these events will have a significant impact on your quality of life. Instead of seeing your challenges as disasters and wallowing in fear or self-pity, what if you recognized them as opportunities for growth? How would your life be different if you decide to use these challenges as stepping stones to even greater success and happiness for yourself?

Why Perseverance is a Super Power

Did you know that you have persevered through many challenging situations throughout your life? Did you also know that perseverance is actually a very natural part of who you are?

You don't believe me? Let me explain.

When you were an infant, you had no idea how to feed yourself. The first few times you tried to feed yourself solid food, you made a complete mess. Chances are you fed your cheeks, chin, nose, and floor more often than you fed your mouth. But you didn't stop, did you? You continued to push forward and now, look at you! You feed yourself effortlessly, and for the most part, you actually put food into your mouth and not on the floor like you once did.

Then, there are those times you tried to learn how to walk. How many times did you work so hard to stand up, only to fall right back down before even taking that first step? You didn't give up then either, did you? You persevered.

There could be several chapters written—or even a whole new book or two—about all of the other things that you have pushed through, which allowed you to become a stronger and better person. You do this daily without giving yourself credit or even noticing most of the time.

How would your life look right now if you had decided at eleven months old that walking was too difficult and that you were too scared of falling and getting hurt again? Chances are the freedom of movement that you now enjoy and take for granted as a natural part of your being wouldn't be available to you.

I know this example might seem ridiculous at first, but this situation is not very different than the challenges you may be facing right now. Think about it. At eleven months old, walking was a very difficult and overwhelming task. Your muscles were not fully developed, nor were they strong enough to support your weight effortlessly. You were just learning how to control your motor skills.

The task of controlling your body that is now so automatic to you required much concentration and effort on your part at eleven months old. It required a tremendous amount of effort to just push yourself up from the floor. In the beginning, each time you got up, you fell right back down.

But you persisted.

And don't forget the countless obstacles—the chairs, the coffee table, the slippery floor—all of which made walking ever so challenging. But each time you fell, you brushed yourself off and tried again. You were determined to figure it out and eventually, you did!

At first, you could only take a wobbly step or two before falling again. But you stayed the course. Soon, your steps became solid and they rapidly evolved into walking longer distances. Ultimately, you even learned how to run.

You might laugh at this example, but that's the power of your perseverance at work. If you had decided to give up on yourself at eleven months old, your life would have been dramatically different—and in this extreme example, be filled with significant challenges as a result.

Not only does perseverance help you achieve your goals and build your confidence and self-worth, but when you persevere, you become healthier mentally.

Spend a moment thinking about how you were affected by a change, challenge, or setback that you worked hard to avoid. What was that experience like? Did you think about it so much that you frequently felt worried, tense, or irritable? When you focused so much of your attention on the thing you wanted to avoid, did you have the mental ability to relax and enjoy yourself? Did you feel so anxious that it was hard for you to focus or to sleep well? How about your relationships? How were they affected when you were filled with stress? How satisfied were you with your life at that moment?

Focusing so much on the problem or what's wrong in your life wreaks havoc on your mental health. When you focus on the present moment and on your strengths, you lessen your stress and your mental health improves.

I'm not going to say that once you've decided to persevere, everything will magically fall into place and become easy. You will still have to put in the work to create the changes you desire and some of the work could be boring or difficult for you.

However, when you face your fear and work toward overcoming your problem, your attitude about it changes. Remember, your subconscious mind is always looking for the next command from you and it will do all it can to give you the experience you ask for.

So, when you think of a situation as overwhelming or as something scary to run away from, your subconscious mind will scan your environment and focus on all the details that could reinforce your feelings of overwhelm and fear. This will make your situation appear even more intimidating.

What experiences would your subconscious mind help you focus on when you think of the same situation with an attitude of, "I have no idea how to solve this, but I am determined to figure it out!"? In this instance, your subconscious mind would focus your attention on ways to solve your problem. Instead of bringing only challenges or obstacles to your awareness, your subconscious mind starts showing you available options. As you begin to see some solutions and possibilities, your stress level drops and your confidence rises.

Perseverance helps you to focus on the big picture while staying in the present moment. Remember, fear is based on your thoughts of the past or future. Being in the moment helps you to release your fear and self-doubt. You can then relax and focus on your strengths, come up with creative solutions, and be open to and accepting of new opportunities.

Things that used to stress you out and cause problems for you in the past don't have to be problems anymore. They can be a great opportunity for growth if you let them.

> Life will continue to throw you curve-balls. How you respond to them will determine your outcome and your satisfaction with life.

How to Destroy Fear and Self-Doubt Using the Power of Perseverance

The good news is that tapping into your Inner Super Power of Perseverance is easier than you think. In fact, if you read the chapters in this book in order, you already know everything you need to know to persevere.

You can cultivate a strong sense of perseverance just by using the power of words alone. However, when you incorporate all the Inner Super Powers you've learned, this task becomes much easier. All you have to do is practice what you've learned so far and you will succeed.

For the next few minutes, think of an obstacle you're currently facing that seems difficult to overcome. Pay attention to the thoughts you're having and how they make you feel. Think of all the reasons you've been telling yourself why this obstacle is so difficult to resolve.

Maybe you've attempted to solve it a few times, but haven't succeeded. Or perhaps you haven't tried to address this problem yet because your fear and self-doubt are too high. Whatever the reason might be, can you see that maybe your inability to solve this issue stems from a lack of self-confidence that prevented you from taking the next step of action and pushing through?

Unleashing your Inner Super Power of Perseverance starts with a powerful mindset of "I believe in myself. I know I can handle anything that comes my way."

But what if you don't believe in yourself and you doubt your ability to handle tough situations? That's OK. Even if you don't fully believe in yourself just yet, know that if you decided to tap into your Inner Super Powers, you could build your self-confidence and self-trust.

Since a powerful mindset is the foundation for perseverance and for achieving any goal, you can start out by tapping into your Inner Super Power of Words and choose Word Filters that build yourself up. How you think, feel, and act are direct results of the Word Filters that you choose.

Take a step back and look at the whole picture. Examine the Word Filters you have been using when you think about the situation. How can you change those words to neutralize them and make them non-threatening to you?

Pay attention to how you've been judging yourself and the people involved. Doesn't it feel heavy and burdensome to carry those feelings with you? You can release that unnecessary weight and give yourself a fresh start by tapping into your Inner Super Power of Forgiveness.

Forgive yourself for the things you may have done (and the things you could have done, but didn't do) that you feel contributed to this situation. Those things are in the past and you can choose a different path moving forward. You can also choose to forgive others and free yourself from that old bond to them that held you back.

Examine the Word Filters you have been using when you think about yourself and your abilities. If you have been using Word Filters that tear you down, you can choose to stop doing that now. Instead, start focusing on your strengths and the things you're good at, even if these things are not related to this particular challenge.

Be kind to yourself by using Word Filters that build up your self-trust, self-confidence, and self-esteem. Tap into your Inner Super Power of Love and do things that relax you, energize you, or motivate you to be your best. Remember to incorporate the Inner Super Power of your Body into your daily life. How you choose to present yourself will strongly influence how you feel about yourself and the situation. Practice holding your body in strong and open positions to increase your confidence.

To persevere, you also need to know your goal. Maybe you don't have the exact outcome in mind at this time and that is fine. You can still take the next step if you know the direction you want to head and have a milestone or two in mind.

Look at the obstacle again. What results do you want to create? Do these results match your values or what's important to you? Do you feel good when you think about achieving these results? Create a plan for overcoming your road blocks and transforming them into opportunities for growth. Tap into your Inner Super Powers of Courage and Imagination and practice achieving your goal with ease.

Remember, you can practice any of these steps in the safety of your Personal Creation Studio until you feel good about them.

When you focus on your strengths and take small, consistent steps toward your goals, you will build up your confidence and your ability to persevere will become stronger every day.

Remember, you already know how to persevere. You've been doing this ever since you were an infant.

All you have to do is put one foot in front of the other, one baby step at a time, and you will find yourself stretching and growing in a way you couldn't have predicted or imagined.

Self-Reflection

1. Before reading this chapter, did you know that perseverance is a very natural part of who you are and that you have persevered through many challenging situations? How does knowing that make you feel differently about yourself?

_____

_____

_____

_____

_____

_____

_____

_____

_____

_____

_____

_____

_____

_____

_____

_____

_____

_____

_____

_____

_____

2. Think of a time when you faced a challenging or difficult situation and you gave up. What Word Filters did you use? How did they hold you back?

_____

_____

_____

_____

_____

_____

_____

_____

_____

_____

_____

_____

_____

3. Look at the Words Filters you wrote for question two. How can you change those words to neutralize them and make them non-threatening for you?

_____

_____

_____

_____

_____

_____

_____

_____

_____

_____

_____

_____

_____

4. Think about three instances where you persevered despite challenges. Write the relevant details below.

_____

_____

_____

_____

_____

_____

_____

_____

_____

_____

_____

_____

_____

_____

_____

_____

_____

_____

_____

_____

_____

_____

_____

_____

_____

_____

_____

_____

_____

_____

5. Examine the three scenarios you wrote down. What qualities or strength did you embrace that allowed you to keep going? What Word Filters did you use? Write these down. These qualities and strengths will help you to persevere in future situations.

_____

_____

_____

_____

_____

_____

_____

_____

_____

_____

_____

_____

_____

_____

_____

_____

_____

_____

_____

_____

_____

_____

_____

_____

_____

_____

_____

_____

Tapping into the ISP of Perseverance

Exercise One:
Creating a Playbook for Your Goal

Since perseverance requires a firm belief in your abilities and persistent actions, let's combine all of your Inner Super Powers to help create a Playbook that you can use over and over again to conquer any goal you might have. Completing your Playbook will help you create a solid action plan and a powerful mindset for success.

Free Workbook

If you don't want to write your answers down in this book, you can get a free companion workbook by visiting **JacquiLetran.com/freeworkbook.** You can print it out or complete it on your computer. (You may be able to complete the workbook on your smart phone or tablet if you have a special pdf reader.)

Step One: Your Goal

Spend the next several minutes thinking about a big goal that you would like to achieve and by what date you would like to achieve it. Focus on the big picture here. We will break it down into smaller steps next.

Here are some examples to get you thinking:

- Academic Goal: Bring grade up from three C's and three B's to four A's and two B's.
- Career Goal: Secure a full-time winter internship at my local Arts Museum.
- Family Goal: Earn mom's trust again.
- Fitness Goal: Complete a half-marathon within three hours.
- Personal Goal: Pass my driving exam and get my driver's license.
- Social Goal: Attend one group get-together each week and be fully present during the interactions.

Now, it's your turn. Write down your goal in one simple sentence by filling in the blanks below. For the sake of this exercise, imagine you are a proficient runner working on completing your first half-marathon and you are creating this Playbook on August 15th, which gives you three months to complete your goal.

Example: *It is November 15th. I have completed my first half-marathon in three hours.*

It is _____ (month/date/year). I am/have_____

_____

_____

Step Two: Your Why

Why is this goal important to you? What does achieving this goal mean to you? How would you feel after achieving this goal? Knowing your "why" will help you to stay motivated when things get tough.

Example: *Achieving this goal is important to me because it will show me that I can accomplish whatever I set my mind to. I would be so proud of myself and my accomplishment.*

Achieving this goal is important to me because

_____

_____

_____

_____

Step Three: Your How

Spend the next few minutes coming up with a plan for achieving your goals. If this is a longer-term goal or a more difficult goal, you might want to break this down into multiple smaller goals along the way.

Next, create three to five actions steps for your first intermediate goal. You don't need to know the whole plan to start taking action. In fact, it is often helpful to start with a few steps in mind and adjust your plans as you make progress.

List your intermediate goals below:

Example:

- *Goal 1: Comfortably complete a 10K run within one hour by September 15 [th]*
- *Goal 2: Complete a half-marathon within four and a half hours by October 15 [th]*
- *Goal 3: Complete a half-marathon within three hours by November 15 [th]*

_____

_____

_____

_____

_____

_____

_____

_____

_____

_____

_____

_____

_____

List the action steps for your first intermediate goal:

Example:

<u>Goal 1:</u> *Comfortably complete a 10K run within one hour by September 15 th*

- *Week 1: run 10K three times a week (untimed)*
- *Week 2: run 10K 3 times a week within two hours*
- *Week 3: run 10K 3 times a week within one hour and thirty minutes*
- *Week 4: run 10K 3 times a week within one hour and ten minutes*

_____

_____

_____

_____

_____

_____

_____

_____

_____

_____

_____

<u>Step Four:</u> Your Who:

Knowing that you have support from others can keep you motivated—especially when things get challenging. Think about your goals and the people in your life.

Do you know someone who is going through the same challenge or has a similar goal? Maybe you two could pair up and be accountability partners? Do you know someone who has recently achieved the results you're looking for? Can you ask that person for advice, or better yet, to mentor you? Do you need resources that someone you know might have access to? Who can act as your cheerleader or confidant?

Make a list of people whom you could reach out to for support and encouragement. Write their names and how they might be able to support you below.

<u>Example:</u>

- *Matt and Mary are running this half-marathon, too. Maybe a running/training partner?*
- *Coach Smith: running coach, mentor*
- *Mom: cheerleader, new shoes, race entry fee*

_____

_____

_____

_____

_____

_____

_____

_____

Be willing to reach out to the people on your list and ask for help.

Unleash Your Inner Super Powers

Now that you have defined your goal and created several solid action steps, let's put your Inner Super Powers to work so you can make it happen!

Inner Super Power of Words

1. When you think about your goals, what fears or concerns do you have? What roadblocks do you see? Write these down below.

Example:

- *I'm afraid that it's going to be a lot of work.*
- *I'm afraid I might injure myself.*
- *I don't have enough discipline.*
- *I don't want to limit what I can eat.*
- *I can't run that far.*

_____

_____

_____

_____

_____

_____

_____

_____

_____

_____

_____

_____

_____

2. Transform your I "can't" or "don't know how to" statements above by adding the word "yet" to the end of your sentence.

Example:

I can't run that far, yet.

_____

_____

_____

_____

_____

_____

3. Create a neutral or positive Word Filter for each of the worries, fears, or concerns that you've identified. Notice how you feel just by changing your Word Filters.

Example:

- *It's going to be exciting to train for this half-marathon.*
- *I am taking the necessary preparations to ensure that I am safe while I run.*
- *I can be disciplined.*
- *I've been wanting to adopt a healthier eating habit.*
- *I can properly train to run a half marathon.*

_____

_____

_____

_____

_____

_____

_____

_____

_____

4. Create three to four ISP Commands that are important to help you reach your goals. Practice these commands at least twice daily.

Example:

- *I am excited and committed to completing my half-marathon in two hours.*
- *I am healthy. My body is healthy. I am taking good care of myself as I train.*
- *I am disciplined.*
- *I am determined to crush this goal!*

_____

_____

_____

_____

_____

_____

_____

_____

_____

_____

Inner Super Power of Your Body

1. Pick one power pose to practice for two minutes daily.
2. As you're thinking about taking the steps to complete your goals, how does your body react? If you notice your body and your energy closing in, what could you choose to do differently with your body?

Example: *When I think about running a half-marathon, I notice a heaviness in my shoulders and I want to cross my arms and shuffle my feet. Instead, I can choose to take deep breaths, allow my shoulders to relax, and stand in a powerful and open way.*

Remember to pay attention to your body language throughout your day. Any time your body wants to close up, choose to open up your body, take a strong stance, and keep your gaze forward or upward.

Inner Super Power of Courage

Look at the action steps you identified in the previous exercise. Determine how you can move forward with small, consistent steps each day. If your first action step seems too big, break it down into micro-steps if you need to.

The key is to push yourself to do something that makes you feel slightly uncomfortable, but not overwhelmed. That is how you stretch your boundaries and grow without triggering fear or self-doubt.

Create a plan of how you can courageously take small, consistent steps daily.

Example:
- *Ask Coach Smith to mentor me.*
- *Eat at least one healthy meal each day.*
- *Learn three new stretching exercises to avoid running injuries.*

_____

_____

_____

_____

_____

_____

_____

_____

_____

Inner Super Power of Forgiveness

If thoughts of past failures or perceived flaws come up as you're thinking about achieving your goals, be willing to forgive yourself. If reaching your goal means having to forgive someone else and letting go of the burden associated with that person, be ready to do just that. Remember to look for the lessons from these incidences to help you grow and become a better person.

When you carry an emotional burden with you, it feels heavy and uncomfortable. Imagine having to carry an extra five pounds with you everywhere you go. How would that make you feel? How motivated would you be to do the work with the excess weight?

As you're thinking about completing your goal, write down any heavy or negative thoughts or feelings you might have about yourself or others. You can refer back to chapter six to set yourself free by tapping into your Inner Super Power of Forgiveness. Be kind to yourself and release this unneeded weight to make room for your success.

Example: _Coach Smith called me out and corrected my form last week in front of everyone, which makes me feel_ *stupid and inferior. I'm afraid to ask for help, but Coach Smith is a really good trainer.*

_____

_____

_____

_____

_____

_____

_____

_____

_____

Inner Super Power of Love

1. Remember to be gentle to yourself as you embark on this journey toward achieving your goal. Any time you catch yourself speaking unkindly about you, forgive yourself and change your Word Filters to be loving, supportive, and encouraging.

2. Spend a few minutes thinking about your goal while paying close attention to things that you love about yourself that can motivate you in achieving your goals. You can either add those to your "I Love Me!" list, or write them below.

Example:
- *I love that my legs are so strong.*
- *I love my dedication to improve my stamina.*

_____

_____

_____

_____

_____

_____

_____
_____
_____
_____
_____
_____
_____
_____
_____
_____
_____
_____

3. What self-love activities are especially important or helpful for you as you work on completing your goals? Write those activities down below and invest at least twenty minutes daily to help you let go of any tension while recharging your battery.

Example:

- *Soak my feet in Epsom salt for fifteen minutes after each training day.*
- *Create a music playlist of songs that inspire me to move and listen to them as I run.*

_____
_____
_____
_____
_____
_____
_____
_____

Inner Super Power of Imagination

Now that you have a complete plan for achieving your goals, let's make it even easier for you to conquer them.

Go into your Personal Creation Studio and imagine that you have thoroughly tapped into your Inner Super Powers and you know you can overcome any problem. Think about how that would look and feel. Vividly visualize yourself being confident, courageous, and persistent in every step you take. Envision yourself achieving your goal with ease. Allow yourself to feel the excitement of your victory and celebrate your success.

Notice how happy you feel and how proud you are of yourself and your accomplishments. Practice visualizing this repeatedly until it feels good to you. Remember, each time you practice being successful, you are reprogramming your subconscious mind to look for evidence of your success.

Write down how you felt as you tapped into your ISP of Imagination and practiced your new skills in your Studio.

Example:
- *I feel ready to conquer my goal.*
- *I'm excited to follow through with the plans in my Playbook.*

_____

_____

_____

_____

_____

_____

_____

_____

_____

_____

_____

_____

_____

_____

_____

_____

_____

_____

_____

_____

Inner Super Power of Perseverance

When you have an attitude of perseverance, you can evaluate your situation and transform any setbacks into incredible learning opportunities for yourself. Remember to look for the lessons as you're working on achieving your goals.

At the end of each intermediate goal, do a quick check to ensure you're on track and readjust your plans accordingly. You can use the same four questions you've learned about in Exercise Two of the ISP of Forgiveness to guide your assessments. Feel free to adjust your Playbook as you discover new information along your journey

Example:

1. What went wrong in this situation: *I missed my goal time by ten minutes for week 4. I had midterms during week 4 and didn't take time out for my self-care activities.*

2. What went right in this situation: *I successfully achieved my goals for the first three weeks. I feel*

strong and confident that I can improve my time with additional practice.

3. What can I learn from this situation: *My self-care activities are important to me and my ability to relax and focus on my goals.*

4. How can I improve the outcome of this situation: *Pay attention to my body and make time to take care of myself. I can also practice visualization in my Studio two to three more times each week. I notice how great I feel after practicing in my Studio.*

Remember to write down your evaluation of your progress at the end of each intermediate goal.

1. What went wrong in this situation?

_____

_____

_____

_____

_____

_____

_____

_____

_____

_____

_____

_____

_____

_____

_____

_____

2. What went right in this situation?

_____
_____
_____
_____
_____
_____
_____
_____
_____
_____
_____
_____
_____
_____

3. What can I learn from this situation?

_____
_____
_____
_____
_____
_____
_____
_____
_____
_____
_____
_____
_____

4. How can I improve the outcome of this situation?

_____

_____

_____

_____

_____

_____

_____

_____

_____

_____

_____

_____

_____

_____

_____

As a bonus, if you want to build-up your self-confidence quickly, remember to celebrate your wins no matter how small they may seem. Make a note of your accomplishments and all those good feelings in your I Love Me! list. If you discovered new ways to show yourself love, add that to your self-care list. When you acknowledge yourself and your abilities, you boost your self-belief, self-confidence, and your courage considerably.

Congratulations on completing your Playbook and creating a plan to Unleash Your Inner Super Powers to achieve your goal. Feel free to adapt this Playbook to any goal you want to achieve. Knowing what you want to accomplish and having a plan of action will help you stay on course and increase your chance of accomplishing what you set out to do.

You are the key to your success! Whenever you need a bit of inspiration, motivation, or courage to proceed ahead, go back and review your Playbook and revisit your Studio to invigorate yourself and recharge your battery with these fantastic feelings.

You now have everything you need to Unleash Your Inner Super Powers to destroy your fear and self-doubt, conquer your goals, and create that epic life you've been dreaming about!

BONUS: Five Simple Steps to Release Your Unwanted Emotions

<u>Step One:</u> Identify Your Feeling

To take control of your feelings, you must first be able to identify it. Are you feeling sad, disappointed, irritated, or angry? Maybe you're feeling insecure, worried, or anxious? Be as specific as you can with your unique feeling and avoid generalizing everything as simply "mad," "sad," or "bad." Instead of saying "mad," get specific. Are you angry, hurt, disappointed, or irritated? For this example, let's say you're feeling scared.

<u>Step Two:</u> Rate Your Feeling

Once you've identified your feeling, go ahead and rate it on a scale of 0 to 10, with 10 being the strongest it could be. For example: "I feel scared and it's rated 8 out of 10 (which indicates you are feeling moderately to severely scared)."

<u>Step Three:</u> Locate Your Feeling

Next, identify where in your body you physically feel this feeling. For example, "I feel scared and I notice that feeling in my stomach."

<u>Step Four:</u> Identify Your Physical Sensation

Pay attention to how your body responds and describe the sensation you notice. Maybe you feel some tightness, heaviness or pain. Perhaps it's a dull ache or a burning sensation. Maybe it feels difficult to breathe or you feel choked up. For example, "I feel scared. It's rated 8/10 and it feels like a sharp pain in my stomach."

Step Five: Releasing Your Negative Feeling

Your breath is very powerful and can help you to let go of your negative emotions quickly. Let's use the example of "*I feel scared. It's rated 8/10 and it feels like a sharp pain in my stomach,*" to demonstrate how to release your emotion with your breath.

Start by closing your eyes and for a moment, allow yourself to feel the sharp pain in your stomach. Notice how uncomfortable that sharp pain is. Notice how the sharp pain is holding you back from having a good day.

Then, take a very slow and deliberate deep breath in as you count from one to four. As you're counting slowly, imagine that you are collecting the sharp pain with your breath. Next, hold your breath for a count of four to contain your emotion. Finally, on purpose, choose to release the pain with your exhale. Breathe out fully and loudly, letting that pain go as the air leaves your body.

Take in another slow deep breath in and imagine yourself collecting even more pain. Hold your breath once more for a count of four, and again, choose to release the pain by breathing out even more deeply and loudly than before.

After two deep and deliberate breaths, allow your breathing to become easy and natural. With every easy breath you take in, imagine yourself picking up more pain. With every easy breath out, you're choosing to release the pain.

As you continue to breathe easily, collecting and releasing your negative emotion, give yourself these ISP Commands: "I choose to let this pain (insert your negative feeling here) go. It feels good to let this pain (your negative feeling) go. I deserve to let this pain (your negative feeling) go. I deserve to be free (or a different positive emotion of your choice)."

After a minute or so, re-evaluate your feelings. How do you feel now? Is that old feeling still there, has it changed into a different feeling, or is it still the same feeling, but much less in intensity? Perhaps it is now a two instead of an eight. You might even find yourself pleasantly surprised to find that old feeling had simply vanished.

If you still have any negative sensations, note its location and rate it again. Then, take another two to three deep breaths just as before, collecting and releasing the negative emotions as you do. Continue this exercise until you no longer feel your negative feeling. Your goal is to be completely free of the negative feeling and take control of your emotions. In the beginning, it might take you several minutes. However, the more you practice, the faster and easier it will be!

You can use this exercise to release any unwanted emotions, regardless of where they came from, not just when you are practicing your ISP Commands.

About the Author

Dear Readers:

If you are a teenager struggling with high stress, anxiety, self-doubt, low-confidence or depressive symptoms, I want you to know that you are not alone. I know because I have been there myself. My name is Jacqui Letran, and I have over seventeen years of experience helping thousands of teens. I know I can help you, too!

I know you're frustrated, scared, and lonely. I was, too. I also know confidence, success, and happiness are achievable because I have successfully freed myself from those old emotions and embraced my life with excitement, confidence, and joy. My goal is to help you understand the power of your mind and show you how you can master it so you can overcome your struggles and step into the magnificence of your own being, just like I did—and just like thousands of others have done using these same techniques.

Who am I and why I care...

My life was rather easy and carefree until I hit my teenage years. Overnight, it seemed that all my friends transformed from girls into women! They began to wear make-up and dress in expensive and sexy clothes. They flirted with boys. Some even flaunted the older boys they were dating in front me. I, on the other hand, remained trapped in my boyish body. And, within the rules of my super-strict mother, wearing make-up, sexy clothes, or going on dates were not options for me.

I felt different and isolated—and I quickly lost all my friends. I didn't know what to say or how to act around others. I felt awkward and left behind, as if I didn't belong anywhere. I just didn't fit in anymore. I became more and more withdrawn as I wondered what was wrong with me. Why didn't I blossom into a woman like all my friends? Why was life so difficult and so unfair?

- **I blamed my mother for my problems.** "If she weren't so strict, I would be allowed to date and have nice, sexy clothes," I thought. At least then, I would fit in and everything would be perfect!
- **I also felt very angry.** My life had taken a turn for the worst—but no one seemed to care or even notice. I started skipping school, began smoking, and getting into physical fights. I walked around with a chip on my shoulder and an "I don't care" attitude.
- **I felt invisible, unimportant and unworthy.** Deep down, I only wanted to be acknowledged and accepted. I wanted to belong. I wanted to be loved.

I thought my wishes were answered when I was sixteen. I meet a man who was five years older than me. He showered his love and affection on me and made me feel as if I were the most important person on earth.

Six months later, I found myself a high school drop-out, pregnant and living on public assistance. I felt more alienated than ever before. Everywhere I went, I felt judged and looked down upon. I felt despair and was certain my life was over. I had no future. I knew I was destined to live a miserable life.

I felt truly alone in the world.

Except I wasn't alone; I had a baby growing inside of me. The day I gave birth to my son and saw his angelic face, I knew that it was up to me to break this cycle of self-destructive thoughts and actions.

That's when everything changed!

I began to read every self-help book I could get my hands on. I was on a mission of self-discovery and self-love. Little by little, I let go of the old beliefs that were holding me back from seeing myself as capable, intelligent, and beautiful.

The more I let go of those old beliefs, the more confident I became and the more I was able to accomplish. It was a powerful lesson in how changing my thoughts actually changed my life.

Six years later, at the age of twenty-three, I earned my master's degree in nursing and became a Nurse Practitioner. Since then, I have dedicated more than sixteen years of my life working in adolescent health. I feel so fortunate to be able to use my gift and passion to help teens build unstoppable confidence and empower them to step into their greatness and take charge of their future.

As I reflect on my painful teen years, I realize how I played a major role in determining my life experiences. My low confidence had paralyzed me from taking action, thus reinforcing my misguided belief that I was somehow different or inferior.

I knew I had to share this knowledge to empower other teens to avoid some of the pain I had personally experienced.

In my seventeen-plus year career specializing in Adolescent Health, I have:

- Established, owned, and operated Teen Confidence Academy, specializing in helping teens overcome stress, anxiety and depressive symptoms without medication or long-term traditional therapy
- Established, owned, and operated multiple "Teen Choice Medical Center" locations
- Become an International Speaker and Multi-Award-Winning Author
- Educated and supported thousands of teens to overcome stress, anxiety and depressive symptoms
- Raised a loving, intelligent, and confident young man (he is my pride and joy)
- Completed post-graduate training in holistic and alternative health and healing methods.

I am deeply passionate about helping teens let go of their barriers so they can see the beauty and greatness within themselves. I believe each of us deserves a life full of health, love, and happiness. I also believe that every person has within them all the resources needed to achieve a beautiful and fulfilling life.

In my younger days, when I was going through my troubled teen years, I needed a place where I could be mentored, where I could learn, reflect, and grow; a place where I could heal and get a proper, healthy perspective of myself, as well as of the world around me. I didn't have that option then, or at least I didn't know where to find it. That's why I am writing this book for you now.

Thousands and thousands of teens are living in quiet desperation right now because they haven't been shown the key to their success. My goal in writing this book is to teach you how to understand your mind so that you can control your thoughts, feelings, and actions.

You are much more powerful than you know. By unleashing the power of your mind, you can be in charge of creating the life that you want and deserve. You deserve to be successful and happy in life.

Let's make it happen!

Jacqui Letran

Acknowledgements

I would like to express a heartfelt thank you to my best friend and husband, Joseph Wolfgram. Without his love, endless hours of revisions, and support, this book would not have been possible. Thank you for patiently listening to me talk about this book endlessly.

To my son, Alan Letran, thank you for being my biggest life teacher and source of endless love.

To my family, thank you for believing in me and cheering me on. It means so much to me to have your love and support.

To my editor, Coral Coons, thank you so much for your professionalism and expert advice. You are a joy to work with.

To all of my clients, teachers, and mentors, whether in a professional relationship or in life experiences, a big thank you for being a part of my life. Your presence in my life has helped me grow and transform from a scared little girl into a confident, healthy, and happy woman.

Last, but not least, I like to express my gratitude to my amazing Beta Readers: Ingrid Abild-Pedersen, Candice Betty, Jacqueline Corley, Ricci DePass, Sally Guyatt, Theresa Hartman, Cristy Mosher, Joan Norton, Kaye A. Peters, Christina Raines, Mercedes Silver, and Lesa Smith . I truly appreciate you. Your feedback is invaluable and has made this book even more applicable and enjoyable for readers.

Connect with Me

I love hearing from my readers.

Please feel free to connect with me at:

Amazon.com/Author/JacquiLetran

www.JacquiLetran.com

Facebook.com/JacquiLetran

Linkedin.com/in/JacquiLetran

Instagram.com/MsLetran

Author@JacquiLetran.com

Leave a Review

Please take a minute to share your thoughts about this book by leaving a review on Amazon or Goodreads. I would truly appreciate it.

Free Book Club Visits

If your book club chooses to read any of the three books from the *Words of Wisdom for Teens Series*, I would love to attend your club's meeting virtually to answer any questions you or your members might have.

You can book your free 30-minute spot by emailing me at Author@JacquiLetran.com. Please put "Free Book Club Visits" in the subject line.

Other Books from the Words of Wisdom for Teens Series

If you want to be in control of your feelings and to let go of things easily, this book is for you. Filled with simple tips and easy-to-follow techniques, you can learn to transform your relationships from those filled with tension and frustration to those complete with trust and acceptance.

Do you believe that life is unfair or that change is impossible? This book helps you to understand how your mind works so you'll have the knowledge and power to take control of your thoughts and feelings. The power to create the life you want is in your hands.

Stop the Bully Within Podcast

After seeing thousands of clients, I noticed a common theme among most of those I help—they are their own biggest bully.

Just pause for a moment and think of the words you say to yourself when you did something wrong or failed at something. Are those loving and supportive words? Would you say those same words to someone you love?

For many people, when they think of a bully, they think of someone outside of them—someone who says and does mean things to cause others pain. Not too many people think about the bully they have within themselves.

I'm on a mission to bring awareness to how damaging this "bully within" can be, as well as to help people learn how to transform that inner critic into their best friend, cheerleader, and personal champion for success.

Launch Date: January 18, 2018

Get Sneak Peaks at
FaceBook.com/StoptheBullyWithin

.

49905771R00129

Made in the USA
Lexington, KY
24 August 2019